MISSION:
LION RESCUE

A lioness sits with several cubs in the high grasses of the Maasai Mara National Reserve in Kenya.

MISSION: LION RESCUE

ALL ABOUT LIONS AND HOW TO SAVE THEM

BY **ASHLEE BROWN BLEWETT** WITH NATIONAL GEOGRAPHIC EXPLORER **DANIEL RAVEN-ELLISON**

NATIONAL GEOGRAPHIC KiDS

WASHINGTON, D.C.

>> CONTENTS

A mischievous young lion looks into the camera after slipping and nearly falling from a tree branch.

Lions, and *Tigers,* and *Polar Bears*—oh, my! Be sure to check out the other titles in the Mission: Animal Rescue series. Coming soon to bookshelves near you.

MISSION: ANIMAL RESCUE

At National Geographic we know how much you care about animals. They enrich our planet—and our lives. Habitat loss, hunting, and other human activities are threatening many animals across the globe. The loss of these animals is a loss to humanity. They have a right to our shared planet and deserve to be protected.

With your help, we can help save animals—through education, through habitat protection, and through a network of helping hands. I firmly believe the animals of the world will be safer with us on their side.

Throughout this book and the other books in the Mission: Animal Rescue series, you'll see animal rescue activities just for kids. If you go online at kids.nationalgeographic.com/mission-animal-rescue, you can join a community of kids who wants to help animals as much as you do. Look for animal rescue videos, chats with explorers, and more. Plus, don't miss the dramatic stories of animal rescues in *National Geographic Kids* magazine.

We share our Earth with animals. Helping them means helping our planet and protecting our future. Together we can do it.

—Daniel Raven-Ellison, *Guerrilla Geographer and National Geographic Explorer*

YOUR PURCHASE SUPPORTS ANIMALS AND THEIR HABITATS

The National Geographic Society is a nonprofit organization whose net proceeds support vital exploration, conservation, research, and education programs. Proceeds from this book will go toward the Society's efforts to support animals and their habitats. From building bomas for big cats to protect their wild territory to studying elephants and how they communicate to exploring wild places to better understand animal habitats, National Geographic's programs help save animals and our world. Thank you for your passion and dedication to this cause. To make an additional contribution in support of Mission: Animal Rescue ask your parents to consider texting ANIMAL to 50555 to give ten dollars. See page 128 for more information.

An African lion charges toward an invading male in the Okavango Delta in Botswana.

We all know that classic lion sound—a thundering roar! But do you know what those roars mean? Humans think of a roar as a powerful symbol, a fearsome noise that makes others stop in their tracks. But lions use their roars as their voice, to communicate with their pride. Lions will roar together or alone and it can mean something as simple as, "It's time to hunt" or as daring as, "Stay back!"

Lions, and their fantastic roars, are common in our modern world. They're in movies, books, and business logos, and their fluffy cubs are adored in pictures and at zoos. We have even adapted the word "lion" in our language to mean more than just the creature. Lions have been a part of human culture for thousands of years, but today they're in trouble.

Though lions are idolized around the world as symbols of the African savanna, they are being driven out of their habitats by hunters, poachers, human encroachment, and more. They are vanishing. And even though, for some reading this book, that may be happening half a world away, it is still an important issue that affects the entire planet. Can you imagine a world without lions?

Together we can save lions. All around the world there are energetic people who care deeply about lions and are taking action to save their lives and habitats. The more of us who care enough to cause an uproar, the more success we'll have in protecting this amazing animal.

At the end of each chapter of this book, you will find a rescue challenge. Every activity will help to cause an uproar and help to save lions, but only if you make your voice heard. Be sure to think of a way to let as many people as possible know about what you have done.

So let out that roar and read on to learn how to make your voice loud. Let's save lions!

>> THROUGH A LION'S EYES

On a dark night in Botswana, Africa, the once distant noises now morph into deep, bellowing roars. To lioness Ma di Tau and her mate, the signal is clear. The pair bristle between long blades of savanna grass, drink in unfamiliar scents, and scan the tree line. They are ready for battle.

MA DI TAU

Suddenly, two massive, fully maned lions from another pride explode out of the thicket and tackle the male. He claws and gnaws in defense of his land, his mate, and their three small cubs hidden in a secret spot for the night.

Amid the chaos, Ma di Tau sprints toward three of the invading females. They quickly pin her to the ground, but with one careful swipe of her claw, Ma di Tau impales the largest attacker's eye. The invaders retreat for now, but their message was delivered: this territory has new rulers.

Wounded and bleeding, Ma di Tau flees, never to see her mate alive again.

The invading pride from the north is not after additional pride members; they want land. Humans moved into their home and pushed them out.

Now Ma di Tau, or "Mother of

MOVIE STAR

Filmmakers Dereck and Beverly Joubert followed Ma di Tau for years, filming her experiences in Africa, and later made a movie from the coverage. The story of Ma di Tau as retold in *Mission: Lion Rescue* is based on Dereck Joubert's screenplay for the film.

AS TOLD BY ACADEMY AWARD® WINNER JEREMY IRONS

THE MOST POWERFUL FORCE IN NATURE IS A MOTHER'S LOVE

THE LAST LIONS

AN INCREDIBLE TRUE STORY OF SURVIVAL

A FILM BY CELEBRATED WILDLIFE FILMMAKERS DERECK & BEVERLY JOUBERT

Ma di Tau stares out over Duba Plains.

Lions," presses farther south toward the wetlands, little ones in tow.

STRUGGLE FOR SURVIVAL

The invading males tail Ma di Tau all the way to the river's edge. She wades in with her cubs close behind, but the smallest one stops. Somehow he knows danger lurks beneath the murky water. The invaders are bearing down on the cub and the family. It's now or never.

Finally, the cub slips into the water. Only now it's too late. The commotion has alerted nearby crocodiles, and the cub disappears with a splash. It's a harsh way for these lions to begin their new lives, and a stark reminder that every day is a fight for survival.

Ma di Tau and her two remaining cubs have escaped to Duba Island, an isolated patch of land in the middle of the Okavango Delta. Its rivers and wetlands promise safety but present new challenges.

To survive, Ma di Tau will need to hunt and kill one of Africa's largest and most aggressive animals: the Cape buffalo. Masterminding a plan to take down one of these behemoths—which can grow to more than twice a lioness's size—all alone won't be easy. She'll have to adapt.

HUNTING IN WATER IS TOUGH BUT HAS GIVEN MANY OF THE DUBA ISLAND LIONS EXTRA-STRONG NECK, CHEST, AND UPPER LEG MUSCLES.

Ma di Tau stalks the herd day and night, scanning for weaknesses. She tries taking a lone calf, but angers the mother buffalo, who fights to fend Ma di Tau off. Next, she tries a very bold, all-out charge on the entire herd, but hopelessly scatters them.

Time passes and Ma di Tau tries a new strategy. The herd is advancing toward the river in the distance. Lions hate water; buffalo know this. They won't suspect an attack there. So Ma di Tau hides her cubs in a nearby thicket and tails the herd to the river. She plucks up some courage and slips undetected into the croc-infested water. She paddles silently across the deep river and then charges through the shallows. This startles the herd into a frantic stampede, and Ma di Tau pounces onto the rump of a lone, straggling cow.

"Mwaaa! Mwaaa!" The distress calls send the herd splashing back to the cow's aid, but amid the chaos Ma di Tau isolates and kills a small calf. Finally, a victory! Soon she'll produce much needed milk for her cubs. But before returning home, she lies down exhausted from the hunt and falls fast asleep.

A NEW PRIDE

The next morning, Ma di Tau returns to the hiding spot, but her babies are gone. They must have wandered off during the night. But where are they now? Ma di Tau panics at the sight of trampled grass and then sees her. Across the open field lying broken in flattened grass is the female cub. There's no sign of the male cub.

Enraged, Ma di Tau charges toward the grazing herd. She lunges at the largest bull, latching onto his neck and mouth. But the nearly one-ton bull easily shakes her to the ground. Ma di Tau gets up, glances across the field, and sees an invader lioness who has been attracted to the commotion. Ma di Tau charges headlong across the plain.

The two proud lionesses fight as a tumbling, dusty ball of rage across the grass. They snarl and swipe their needle-like claws. Ma di Tau finally pins the other to the ground, but her rampage doesn't stop. With fire in her eyes she advances toward the buffalo herd once more. And this time the other lionesses follow. After this epic show of strength, Ma di Tau has become the leader of the lioness invaders.

But something steals Ma di Tau's attention from the buffalo—a faint but familiar whimper. She lowers her head and scours the horizon. Through a tangle of bony legs and pointed buffalo horns, she spots him. Her male cub—alive and well!

Ma di Tau charges at the herd, putting distance between them and her defenseless cub. The other lionesses flank Ma di Tau for reinforcement. Together, they push the herd into retreat.

In that moment, a new pride was born. And after great loss and a desperate struggle for survival, a wave of hope emerges for this courageous mother and her sole surviving cub.

Ma di Tau crouches low in front of a herd of Cape buffalo. In order to feed herself and her two cubs, Ma di Tau must learn to hunt this fearsome enemy.

CHAPTER 1

>> KING OF BEASTS

"A LION SLEEPS IN THE HEART OF EVERY BRAVE MAN."
— TURKISH PROVERB

Lions know what it feels like to be King. Born from the red dust of sub-Saharan Africa, they've reigned over the continent for hundreds of thousands of years, demanding awe and respect alike from anyone that crosses their path.

A NATURAL LEADER

Scientists call these regal cats *Panthera leo,* the second largest feline in the cat, or Felidae, family. Cats are mammals—they're coated in various textures and shades of hair, give birth to live young, and suckle their cubs or kittens for their first few weeks or months on Earth. And all cats, big or small, are carnivores—meat-eaters uniquely designed to hunt and kill their food.

A cat's natural instinct is to kill. They're born with it—even the cuddly kitten, just new to the world.

Free-range, domestic house cats kill billions of birds, mice, and other small rodents every year—even driving some to extinction. How do they do that? It's because cats have evolved some very specific, and powerful, adaptations.

Sharp vision, heightened hearing, and a keen sense of smell allow these fearsome predators to accurately home in on prey—whether in your own backyard, among noisy city streets, or even in swampy wetlands filled with lots of different animal scents and thick mud. Felines are also armed with fierce weaponry. Razor-sharp, retractable claws easily pierce tough, leathery skin; powerful jaws grasp and choke prey; and long, dagger-like teeth snag and rip into flesh.

From pint-size tabby cats to the Amur tiger, 37 different species make up the Felidae family. But lions are part of a more exclusive group: the *big* cats.

FEMALES PREFER MALE LIONS WITH THE LONGEST AND DARKEST MANES.

Two lions greet each other on the Maasai Mara National Reserve. When greeting, lions rub their cheeks and sometimes even their necks and bodies against each other.

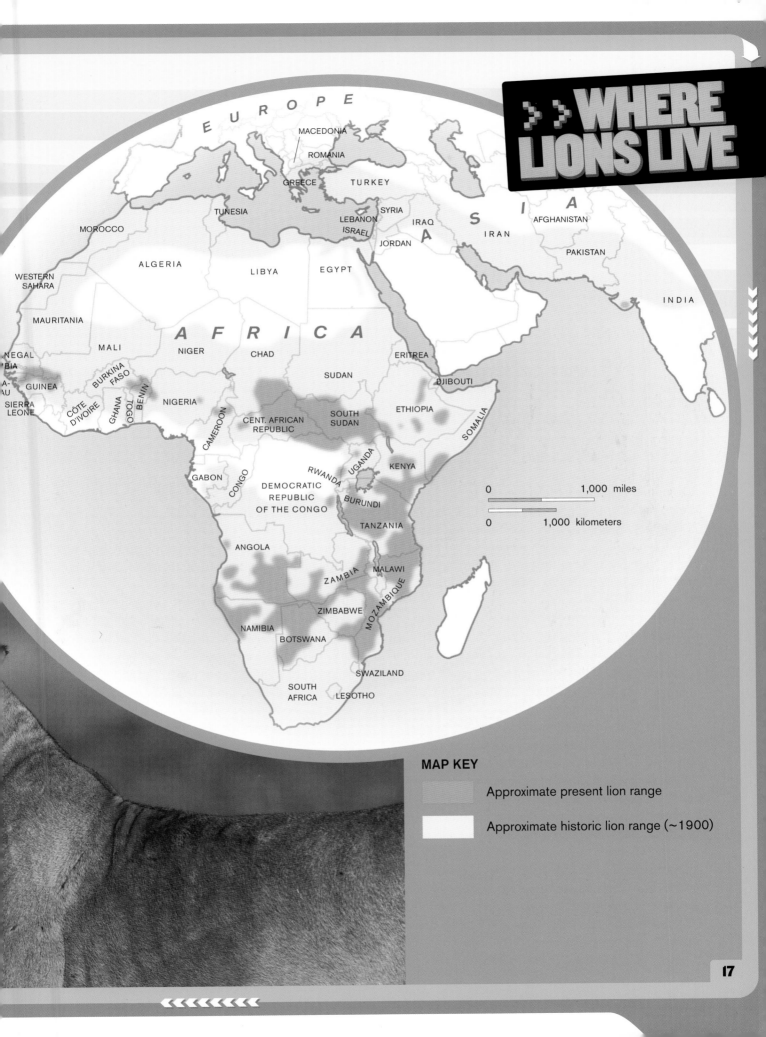

EUROPE

MACEDONIA

ROMANIA

GREECE TURKEY

TUNISIA

LEBANON SYRIA

ISRAEL IRAQ

JORDAN

A S I A

AFGHANISTAN

IRAN

PAKISTAN

MOROCCO

ALGERIA LIBYA EGYPT

WESTERN
SAHARA

INDIA

MAURITANIA

A F R I C A

MALI NIGER CHAD

ERITREA

NEGAL
BIA

SUDAN

DJIBOUTI

GUINEA

BURKINA
FASO

A-
AU

CÔTE
SIERRA D'IVOIRE
LEONE

GHANA

TOGO
BENIN

NIGERIA

CAMEROON

CENT. AFRICAN
REPUBLIC

SOUTH
SUDAN

ETHIOPIA

SOMALIA

GABON

CONGO

RWANDA UGANDA

DEMOCRATIC
REPUBLIC
OF THE CONGO

BURUNDI

KENYA

ANGOLA

TANZANIA

ZAMBIA MALAWI

ZIMBABWE

MOZAMBIQUE

NAMIBIA

BOTSWANA

SWAZILAND

SOUTH
AFRICA LESOTHO

0 1,000 miles

0 1,000 kilometers

MAP KEY

Approximate present lion range

Approximate historic lion range (~1900)

The titles "big cat" and "roaring cat" describe the genus *Panthera*, which includes lions, tigers, leopards, and jaguars. Big cats can make a range of noises, including—thanks to unique throat anatomy—their distinctive roar. One of the most terrifying sounds to echo through any habitat, roaring helps large prides of lions scare smaller prides away from their highly desirable territories.

BUILT TOUGH

Fear is probably not something that comes easily to a lion. From nose to tail, a male lion's muscular body can stretch up to ten feet (3 m) long and weigh over 500 pounds (227 kg). Picture a cat the size of your living room sofa stalking through your house. Shaggy manes cloak adult male lions' necks, which darken as the animals age to an almost black color. A bulky mane stands out against open grasslands, warning other male lions that this territory is taken.

Lions are social cats that typically live and hunt in prides. Prides comprise anywhere from a few individuals to 40 or more. They reign over vast territories. A male lion's main job is to protect his pride from invaders, like neighboring prides or bachelor male lions plotting to dethrone a King.

Female lions, called lionesses, are slightly smaller than male lions, and they have no mane. But a sleek, tan-colored frame is the perfect camouflage for a huntress on the prowl—fitting since lionesses do most of the hunting for a pride. Lions are lean, mean, fighting machines that can take down prey more than twice their size. A lone female can pull down a zebra by herself.

Though lions are natural hunters, taking down an animal more than twice their size isn't easy. And it isn't without risk. Lions must often work together to avoid getting hurt. You don't challenge a nearly one-ton Cape buffalo without suffering a swipe of the horns or kick of the hoof every once in a while. But lions don't kill for

A LION IS CALLED *TAU* IN BOTSWANA, *SIMBA* IN KENYA, AND *SHER* IN INDIA.

LIONS ROAR AND SPRAY MIXTURES OF URINE AND OTHER SECRETIONS ON TREES AND BUSHES TO MARK THEIR TERRITORIES.

fun; they kill to live another day. And it's because of their place in the food chain that lions fulfill a crucial role in their ecosystems.

KEYSTONE SPECIES

Every species in an ecosystem works to maintain a healthy homeland. Removing a species is like pulling on a loose thread in your favorite sweater—one tug and you could end up with no sweater and a pile of yarn. If even one species disappears it's enough to weaken a habitat. But if a *keystone* species is removed, an entire ecosystem could collapse.

For a real-life example, we move to North America. Wolf populations once thrived in Yellowstone National Park in the northwestern plains of the United States. But wolf-removal programs and overhunting drove these great predators to local extinction. Shortly after the wolf's disappearance, Yellowstone park rangers noticed something strange. The habitat was breaking down.

Wolves primarily prey on elk, keeping them alert and on the move. After the wolves disappeared, the elk became lazy, gorging themselves on their favorite snack—lush foliage from aspens, willows, and cottonwood trees lining the riverbanks. The elk grazed the trees to death. Songbirds lost their homes, an important food source for beavers vanished, and without healthy tree roots to anchor the soil that makes up riverbeds, the water began to eat away at the banks.

Ecosystems can have more than one keystone species. Take African savannas, for example, where lions roam. Elephants eat small acacia trees. They kick up the trees with their feet and crunch them with their powerful teeth. If elephants disappeared, acacia trees would sprout tall and the savannas would transform into forests. That's a huge change not all animals could adapt to. Zebras, antelope, and other herd animals that depend on savanna grass for food would die. These herd animals feed lions, and without them lions would go hungry.

ZIHRA THE WHITE LION

Zihra is unique. People sometimes think she's albino. But she isn't. Albino animals have no pigment—their hair is pure white, and their eyes are pink. White lions' fur varies from blonde to white. They also have gold or blue eyes, black noses, and black spots on the backs of their ears. Zihra is an African lion, but her parents both carried a rare "white lion" gene. That's how Zihra inherited her special coloring.

Wild white lions are believed to exist in only one place on the planet—the Timbavati region of South Africa. To the local people, white lions are sacred. But by 1994, all the wild white lions had vanished. Greedy people captured the lions and bred them in captivity. They forced white lions into zoos, circuses, and canned hunting camps—where people pay money to hunt animals in small enclosures. The Global White Lion Protection Trust rescued Zihra's mother, Marah, from one of these canned hunting camps. Later, they released Marah, Zihra, and Zihra's two brothers back into the wild on private land in Timbavati. Eventually, more rescue lions joined them, and in 2009, Zihra gave birth to the first wild-born white lions in 18 years.

19

EXPLORER INTERVIEW

MATT BECKER

BORN: USA, GREW UP IN MONTANA
JOB: CEO/PROGRAM MANAGER, ZAMBIAN CARNIVORE PROGRAMME
JOB LOCATION: ZAMBIA
YEARS WORKING WITH LIONS: 5+
MONTHS A YEAR IN THE FIELD: 10

How are you helping save lions?

We study lions in three different ecosystems in Zambia in order to determine how they are faring and what is threatening them. We also take steps to address and minimize these threats. That ranges from removing poachers' snares that catch lions and their prey, to increasing protection of lion habitat and populations, to vaccinating domestic dogs against rabies so they don't transmit it to big cats, to reintroducing lions where they have been depleted.

Favorite thing about your job?

I love helping to train, educate, and give opportunities to the local Zambian students we work with, who will be responsible for ensuring that the Zambian Carnivore Programme's work continues in the long term.

Best thing about working in the field?

There are no fences where we work, thus the animals are free to come and go wherever they please. So we have all sorts of wildlife roaming around camp all day and night—anything from elephants rubbing against your tent frame to spitting cobras behind the toilet!

Worst thing about working in the field?

Living out in the field doesn't allow for a lot of variety besides work, and it's tough to be away from my family and friends for long stretches.

How can kids prepare to do your job one day?

Find out what it is you love to do and hold onto that. If that something is wildlife conservation, you can pursue an education in wildlife biology or conservation and get as much experience in working with animals on whatever projects you can. Work hard, study hard, and be prepared, but most important don't give up easily and don't get discouraged, as you are capable of doing whatever you want!

Liuwa Plain, one of the places we work, lost all its lions except for one due to human poaching and conflict with lions. In 2011, we helped capture and reintroduce two young lionesses from another Zambian national park to Liuwa Plain. Once a sight only in historical photographs, lion prides can now be seen and heard in Liuwa again.

Wildlife researcher Matt Becker watches over a sedated lion as he tracks their population in Zambia.

LIONS ARE AFRICA'S KEY

If large predators like lions, hyenas, and leopards disappeared, herd populations would balloon, and grazers of all kinds would eat up the grass. This time, instead of the savannas turning into forests, they would become sandy deserts.

Humans play a major role in habitat health too. Humans knock down trees to build homes and buildings. They convert grassland to farmland. And they build roads and highways that cut through animals' homes. This is especially troublesome for lions.

When you're a big cat, everything is supersize. Their territories are massive. Depending on the size of the

>> **EXPERT TIPS**

Lion-tracker and scientist Philipp Henschel's tips on looking for lions:

1 The famous Indian wildlife biologist Dr. Ullas Karanth once said, "if you want to study tigers, you have to learn to think like a tiger." The same holds true for lions.

2 Think about what a lion needs to survive: prey animals, enough vegetative cover to conceal him when stalking his prey, drinking water, safety from humans, and more.

3 Once you internalize those needs and start to read the landscape with the eyes of a lion, you will also be able to find lions and study them successfully.

A young male lion crosses paths with an elephant in Tshukudu Game Reserve in South Africa.

SEARCHING FOR LIONS IN GABON

Most people would cringe at the thought of camping for weeks in the African bush—with its extreme heat, biting bugs, and no running water. But to Philipp Henschel, there's nothing better. Philipp works for Panthera, an organization dedicated to saving big cats. He scours remote African wilderness in search of critically threatened lion populations. Then he persuades local governments to take action to save them.

On one expedition, Philipp hiked for many weeks and hundreds of miles across Gabon's Batéké Plateau—a vast, savanna thought to be Gabon's last lion stronghold. He searched tirelessly for dusty lion paw prints, scat, and scratch marks. But sadly no lions remained. Philipp thought the Gabonese government would surely give up hope. Surprisingly, they decided to protect Batéké Plateau, hoping that one day they could reintroduce lions. It's been a slow recovery, but today buffalo and other lion prey populations in Batéké Plateau National Park are on the rise. Philipp hopes that lions will soon be heard again roaring through the plateau.

Check out Panthera at panthera.org.

Philipp Henschel goes on a trek to conduct a lion field survey.

pride, and the type and amount of prey available, lion territories range from 8 square miles (21 sq km) to more than 400 square miles (1,036 sq km). That's a lot of land. But it's swiftly being pulled out from under their paws.

The human population has exploded to seven billion over the past several decades. People are moving into lion territory and pushing the lions out at an alarming rate. In addition to habitat loss, lions are poached, killed by farmers, and hunted for trophies.

It's estimated that in the early 1800s, more than one million lions roamed throughout Africa and Asia. Today, only a fraction of that number remains. The modern lion population is scattered across isolated plots of land in Africa—a vast continent they once dominated—and currently one small forest in India. Rapidly shrinking ranges also means more competition for land and food among lions. More and more lions are crossing paths, and they don't play nice. Lions risk their lives to defend their homes.

HUMANS VS. LIONS

The King of Beasts has fended off threats to its crown for thousands of years, but humans are an enemy that now outnumbers the lion 200,000 to 1. To some, it may seem removing one measly lion out of thousands wouldn't make a difference. But removing a male lion is devastating to a pride. When a male lion is shot or poisoned, his entire pride becomes vulnerable to outside attacks. Continually killing the pride males could actually cause the whole pride to disappear.

Over the past 100 years, the lion population has plummeted from approximately hundreds of thousands to as few as 35,000 today. It's estimated that for every one billion people we add to the human population, the lion population gets cut in half. If we continue on this path, lion numbers could drop to as few as 17,000 individuals in the next decade.

But there is hope.

Several organizations and individual experts are taking action. They're working directly with the people who affect lions' lives, including local governments, villagers, and farmers. With support from the National Geographic Society, Explorers-in-Residence Dereck and Beverly Joubert founded the Big Cats Initiative to halt the decline of big cats and fund cat-based conservation projects. There are explorers trekking across Africa to count lions and map their ranges, and many other initiatives around the world.

Ma di Tau was a special case. Although humans pressured other lions into taking her land, and she lost her mate and two of her cubs, she received a second chance. She won over the Tsaro Pride, giving her and her male cub another shot at life. Other lions may not be so lucky.

The time is now. We can coexist. Let's save lions!

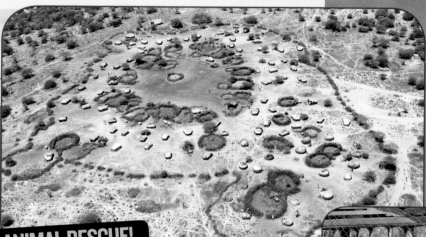

Left: Large bomas inside Samburu National Park in Kenya help keep livestock and lions safe. Below: A villager stands next to a reinforced boma.

>> ANIMAL RESCUE!

BUILDING BOMAS

Nighttime in Maasailand—an area that surrounds the Maasai Mara Game Reserve in Kenya, Africa—is prime hunting time for lions. There the lions encounter easy targets—penned-in cows, sheep, and goats. But killing livestock puts the lions' lives in danger, because the Maasai retaliate. Anne Kent Taylor has worked on conservation projects in this area for 13 years. Local rangers nicknamed her Chuma Za Zamani, which means "old steel" in Swahili. Anne was determined to help solve the Maasai's lion problem, while keeping villagers, their livestock, and the lions safe.

Working closely with the local communities in the Transmara district, Anne began a project to install unbreakable chain-link fencing around the livestock enclosures, called bomas. So far, the Anne K. Taylor Fund has helped install more than 350 of these structures and they have proved to be extremely successful. Anne has even extended the boma project to neighboring districts, including Mara North Conservancy and Olare Orok Conservancy. Her goal is to see as many bomas as possible protected in Maasailand.

Check out Anne's work at aktaylor.com.

A lioness strolls with her cubs through tall grass.

>> RESCUE CHALLENGE

MAKE A LION

Lions live far away from most of us. They are so distant that they're invisible to many of us and can be easily forgotten. By doing this challenge, you'll be putting lions on the map for all to see. When someone asks about the lion you made, this is your opportunity to explain the problems lions face!

NOVICE

DRAW A LION IN A PUBLIC PLACE. There are lots of different ways that you could do this. You could:

USE A LARGE SHEET OF PAPER OR WALLPAPER. This way you can draw your lions in secret before putting them on display.
DRAW ON SHEETS USING FABRIC PENS. Sheets can be folded up, moved around easily, hung up, turned into flags, and used again.

CHALK YOUR LIONS ON A WALL OR PAVEMENT. Chalk comes in lots of colors and is a cheap way to go big. Ask an adult for permission before you chalk anything!
GO NATURAL AND USE LEAVES, sand, or pebbles to draw your lion.

EXTREME

READY FOR A SUPERSIZE CHALLENGE? Create a picture of a lion that can be seen from space. Can you get your image photographed by a passing aircraft or satellite?

The bigger your lion, the more likely it is that it will be seen. To successfully achieve this challenge you will need to:

MAKE A LIFE-SIZE, TEN-FOOT (3-M)-LONG LION OUT OF FREE STUFF YOU CAN FIND. Large cardboard boxes are light and great for decorating. If you go exploring, you should be able to find all kinds of interesting things—from sticks and leaves to clean trash. Decorate your lion with a mane, sharp teeth, and vicious claws. Would you roam with a regal male, or a female huntress?

1. Team up with as many people as you can; this is a big job!

2. Plan your lion drawing in advance. You could create a grid or map that will show people where to draw each part of the lion.

3. Find a big open space—like an empty field or public park—with a clear view of the sky.

4. Pick a place where nobody will disturb you, at least for a while.

5. Get under a flight path if you can, so that passengers can see your lion.

6. Choose the best material to draw your lion. If you are in the desert or on a beach this could be in the sand. Or you could think long term and seed plants in soil to grow in the pattern of a lion.

7. Finally, tell people flying over your lion to look down! A great way to do this is by contacting your local news.

CHAPTER 2

>> LAND OF LIONS

"TO SIT AND LISTEN TO A LION ROAR IN THE AFRICAN BUSH IS TO SIT ON THE EDGE OF PARADISE, A WILDERNESS THAT IS BOTH RARE AND ESSENTIAL."

– DERECK JOUBERT, NATIONAL GEOGRAPHIC EXPLORER-IN-RESIDENCE

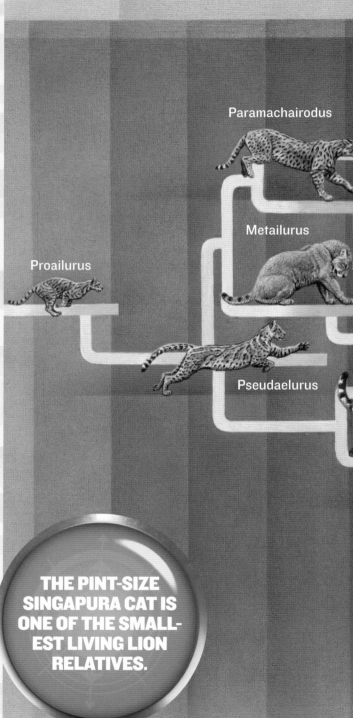

The cat family tree through the ages. Evidence of coexistence between lions and humans dates back more than 30,000 years to ancient caves in Europe.

OLIGOCENE
33.9–23.5 million years ago

MIOCENE
23.5–5.2 million years ago

Paramachairodus

Metailurus

Proailurus

Pseudaelurus

Lions and the other 36 cat species, including your own furry feline, all evolved from one small, catlike creature called *Proailurus. Proailurus* ranged across Europe and Asia 30 million years ago. About twice the size of a modern house cat, they dwelled primarily in trees and used their flexible wrists to grab low-hanging branches. Then, 12 million years ago, *Proailurus* headed to the ground and the cat family split into two branches, or types, of cats: large cats, and small and medium-size cats.

CAT TYPES

Small and medium-size cats make up the majority of the Felidae family, with about 30 species. These smaller cats include everything from common house cats to cheetahs. Big cats complete the Felidae family. The big four "roaring cats" are lions, tigers, leopards, and jaguars. Some cats—like lions—are divided into subspecies.

Subspecies form when groups of animals from the same species separate. If food is scarce or space is limited, some individuals will abandon their homes and move to another part of the world. Natural events separate animals, too.

Ground-shattering earthquakes sometimes send mountain peaks spiking up through the ocean. Or broad sheets of earth collapse into giant sinkholes. These events scatter animals into isolated groups around the new landform. The groups no longer mate with each other, and their new habitats influence their evolution. Over time, the groups begin to exhibit unique characteristics, develop distinct genes, and become subspecies.

AFRICAN LIONS (PANTHERA LEO LEO)

Most people picture Africa when they think of lions. That's because today most of the world's wild lions live there. Lions evolved in Africa just like humans did. We have coexisted for more than 30,000 years—battling each other for land and food since the beginning. But

THE PINT-SIZE SINGAPURA CAT IS ONE OF THE SMALLEST LIVING LION RELATIVES.

PLIOCENE
5.2-1.6 million years ago

PLEISTOCENE
1.6 million-10,000 years ago

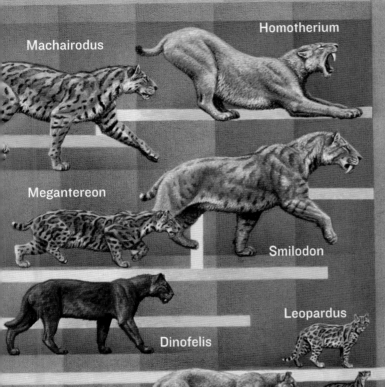

Machairodus

Homotherium

Megantereon

Smilodon

Dinofelis

Leopardus

Puma

Felis

Miracinonyx

Acinonyx

Panthera

GENETICALLY RELATED CATS

Ocelot lineage
7 species

Domestic cat lineage
7 species

Puma lineage 3 species

PANTHERINES
Panther lineage 6 species
Lynx lineage 5 species
Rusty-spotted cat lineage
 1 species
Caracal lineage 2 species
Bay cat lineage 2 species
Asian leopard cat lineage
 4 species

NEARLY HALF OF THE WORLD'S WILD LIONS LIVE IN TANZANIA.

An African lion faces gritty wind head-on in the Nossob Riverbed in Kalahari Gemsbok National Park in South Africa.

about 150 years ago, two things tipped the scales in the humans' favor: numbers and guns.

Back then lions dominated the African landscape—their territories stretched from north of the Sahara desert to the South African Cape. But the total worldwide human population had hit one billion, and guns were being mass-produced for the first time. Toward the end of the 19th century, Europeans took control of most of the land in Africa. They tilled land to plant crops. And they hunted lions' natural prey to eat for themselves. People also hunted lions and other big cats for sport.

>> ANIMAL RESCUE!

SHIVANI BHALLA

Shivani Bhalla moved to Samburu—a community area in the Ewaso Nyiro ecosystem in northern Kenya—more than ten years ago to study lions. In 2007, she founded the Ewaso Lions Project. Working together with the local people who share land with the big cats, Shivani develops new conservation strategies to save lions.

Three years ago, the project teamed up with several Samburu warriors to create Warrior Watch. Today, 17 warriors help track and map the movements of resident lion prides and individual lions. The warriors also educate their friends and family on why lions are important. Warrior Watch has been so successful that Shivani is launching a new program to include community elders.

Samburu children benefit from Shivani's project, too. Ewaso Lions takes local children on wildlife safaris, and it recently began a wildlife camp for children. It also donated more than 800 books to create the Simba Library at the local primary school. One of the books—*Simba Stories*—the children wrote themselves. Its pages are filled with their drawings, poems, and stories about lions. Shivani is hopeful that these students—and the people who read their book—will grow up to be the next generation of Samburu's wildlife ambassadors. To learn more about Ewaso Lions, visit ewasolions.org.

Shivani Bhalla takes measurements on a sedated lion.

Most European rulers returned control of their African territories to the local people by the mid-1990s, but villagers continued to hunt and clear land. People have destroyed more than a million square miles (2.2 million sq km) of African savannas in the past 50 years, forcing lions into remnants of their once massive territories. Now, instead of ranging the entire continent, Africa's lions inhabit four regions: West, Central, East, and Southern Africa. Their current range map looks more like a scattered battle zone than a secure homeland.

LION STRONGHOLDS

Most of Africa's lions live in protected parks and game reserves in East and Southern Africa. For now, prey populations in the parks are healthy, and lions that live there are doing well. These areas are the strongholds. Lands outside these parks are battlefields.

Poaching—killing animals without permission—and human settlement have devastated lion populations in West and Central Africa. People wiped out more than half of the healthy lion populations there in just five years. Only about 2,500 lions remain in Central Africa. Fewer than 500 lions cling to tattered territories in West Africa.

The rest of Africa's free-ranging lions—about 3,000—live outside protected parks in the East and South. Conflicts there are increasing. Homes, roads, and farms crisscross lion territories. And food is scarce. Some free-range lions die of hunger. Desperate lions wander into villages to look for food—a risk that can turn deadly for both lions and humans.

CONFLICT IN TANZANIA

The most devastating example of human-lion conflict in Africa is in southern Tanzania. People converted most of the savanna to farmland for rice, corn, and cassava (a root vegetable that looks like a sweet potato). And they built small villages.

With little grass left to eat, the lions' natural prey moved on or died out. And bushpigs moved in, raiding farmers' crops at night.

But fat, tasty-looking bushpigs also attract lions, luring them into human territory. Lions slink through the fields at night looking for bushpigs. But if a starving lion encounters a lone human, it won't hesitate to

Skull of *Panthera atrox*, the extinct "American lion" that lived in western North America and South America during the Pleistocene era.

THE AMERICAN LION

In 1979, Alaskan gold miners discovered a 36,000-year-old mystery: a 1,500-pound (680-kg) Alaska steppe bison *(Bison priscus)* called Blue Babe frozen in Ice Age–permafrost. At first, Blue Babe's death was a mystery, but as the bison thawed, clues appeared. Deep, gaping scratches on his rump and punctures on his snout suggest Blue Babe died at the claws of a fierce predator: the American lion *(Panthera atrox)*.

Panthera atrox ranged across North America and Mexico until about 10,000 years ago. It resembled modern lions, but *Panthera atrox* weighed as much as 750 pounds (340 kg)! That's 250 pounds (113 kg) heavier than a male African lion today! American lions likely lived and hunted in open grasslands like their modern cousins, but Ice Age winters were brutal. A large tooth fragment wedged in Blue Babe's neck hints that his body froze before the predators could finish him off.

AFRICAN VS. ASIATIC LIONS

AFRICAN LIONS		ASIATIC LIONS
Females: up to 400 pounds (181 kg) Males: up to 550 pounds (248 kg)	**SIZE**	Females: up to 260 pounds (118 kg) Males: up to 420 pounds (190 kg)
Males have a mane that darkens as they age Almost no elbow fur tufts, short tail tuft	**PHYSICAL TRAITS**	Males have short mane, ears are always visible Large fold of skin underneath belly area Thick fur on elbows, long tail tuft
Zebra, wildebeest, Cape buffalo	**PREY**	Chital deer, small mammals
35,000 (estimated)	**CURRENT POPULATION**	400

An African lion cub clings to the back of an adult lion in the Okavango Delta in Botswana.

attack. Starving lions have also been known to sneak into villages on moonless nights and *stalk* humans. They seek out lone stragglers. And they pounce.

One September evening in 2001, in southern Tanzania's Lindi district, an eight-year-old girl named Pili Tengulengu was nabbed by a lion. She and her cousins had been playing near their home. On their return, the children cut through a patch of tall grass on a well-worn path. Pili lagged behind. Suddenly, a lion sprang out of the grass, grabbed Pili, and took off. Stories like this are not uncommon here. Between 1998 and 2009, lions attacked more than 1,000 people in southern Tanzania. The attacks continue today, and humans often kill the aggressive lions.

Man-eating lions usually occur only where natural prey is scarce or when a lion is sick or injured. But even when prey exists, lions and humans that share land often still conflict.

WARRIORS SHARING LAND

The Maasai people of East Africa populate the Great Rift Valley that straddles northern Tanzania and southern Kenya. They herd goats and cattle, and they also live in mud huts alongside lions. The

Maasai have strong warrior traditions. Lions don't prey on the Maasai people, but they do kill and eat their livestock—especially in the dry season, when most of the lions' natural prey has migrated to far-off watering holes.

But taking a cow or goat from the Maasai is like stealing their money—and the Maasai don't tolerate thieves. "I will protect my father's cattle from lions," said one 15-year-old warrior in training. "If a lion kills one of our cows, I will kill it." Maasai warriors traditionally organize hunting parties to track and spear lions that kill their cattle.

It's easy to empathize with a person when lions take their family and their livestock. And it makes sense why lions that do live in parks fight to stay there. But lions are losing ground. Even some of Africa's protected parks, where many lions live, are getting smaller. They can't protect all of Africa's lions. Unless more people take action soon, lion deaths will continue to rise.

ASIATIC LIONS (*PANTHERA LEO PERSICA*)

Panthera leo persica is the African lion's slightly smaller, shaggier cousin. African and Asiatic lions split into two subspecies about 100,000 years ago. But like their

ANIMAL SUPERPOWERS

LION SPEAK

LIONS ROAR TO COMMUNICATE WITH THEIR PRIDEMATES AND TO ANNOUNCE THEIR PRESENCE IN A TERRITORY.

LIONS CAN COUNT THE NUMBER OF NEARBY LIONS JUST BY LISTENING TO THEIR ROARS.

BY LISTENING TO ROARS, LIONS KNOW WHETHER A LION IS A FRIEND OR AN INVADER AND EVEN IF IT'S A MALE OR FEMALE!

Tourists riding in safari jeeps photograph a male Asiatic lion in Gir Forest National Park in India.

Asiatic lions drink from a man-made watering hole in Gir Forest National Park. Water in the park is scarce, so forest staff replenish a network of drinking pools for the wildlife.

African counterparts, Asiatic lions' recent history with humans is rocky.

Sport hunting and guns spread across Asia much earlier than in Africa. Kings, princes, and international visitors hunted lions, tigers, and other animals for fun. In the 1600s, Mughal Emperor Jahangir killed more than 17,000 animals in India, including 86 lions and tigers. And British Colonel George Acland Smith shot more than 300 lions in only two years, from 1857 to 1858.

Then Europeans took control of land in India. People demolished forests and used the timber to build railroads and buildings. The new government ordered venomous snakes and other "dangerous beasts" killed in order to protect workers. India's forests and much of its wildlife vanished. By the early 1900s, wild Asiatic lions survived in only one small forest—the Gir Forest— on India's Saurashtra peninsula.

But as Saurashtra's population rose, people leveled large patches of the Gir Forest to make room. The lions slowly disappeared until as few as 20 remained. Luckily, an Indian prince from the Junagadh region of Saurashtra took notice—and he put his royal foot down. The prince declared the Gir

"LIONIZE" MEANS TO TREAT A PERSON LIKE THEY ARE VERY IMPORTANT, LIKE A CELEBRITY.

A male Asiatic lion rests in the shade to escape the extreme heat of India.

lions protected. No one could hunt them without his express permission.

Eventually, Europeans returned control of India's land to its people who banned lion hunting for good. Today, more than 400 Asiatic lions rove in and around the Gir National Park and Wildlife Sanctuary in what is now the Indian state of Gujarat.

THE GIR FOREST

The park and sanctuary comprise 725,000 square miles (1.9 million sq km) of densely forested valleys, rocky hilltops, and grassy plains. Leopards, buffalo, hyenas, and crocodiles dominate the land like they do in Africa. Gazelles, blue bulls, and several species of deer graze on dense forest vegetation. Langur monkeys share the tree canopy with over 300 bird species. For now lions are still King, though they face daily challenges that threaten their survival.

The Gir Forest has hit its maximum lion carrying capacity. Some are fleeing to look for new territories, but the ones that move outside the park face unnatural terrain.

About 150,000 people live in villages around Gir Forest. The local people primarily farm crops and raise livestock. Lions wandering outside the park often get shocked by electric fences. Others get hit by cars or trains, while some fall into open wells.

Fortunately, the people that live in and around Gir Forest are fiercely proud of their lions and rarely kill lions that eat their livestock. For now, they are tolerant. But people continue to alter the land outside the forest. It will soon be cluttered with more homes, businesses, and roads—deadly obstacles for lions on the move. Increased skirmishes between humans and lions are inevitable. These lions need a second home, and fast.

Poorly constructed livestock enclosures, or bomas, offer little protection from the recovering lion population in Waza National Park.

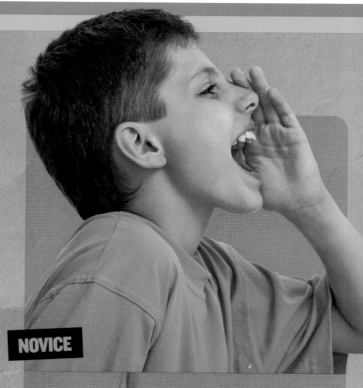

>> RESCUE CHALLENGE

HELP LIONS BE HEARD

Lions can be seen in many statues, crests, and logos. You will also discover lots of companies, brands, and currencies using lions as symbols. Explore the Internet with an adult, and you will soon find lots of people using images of lions in different ways. This is because countries and businesses have historically held lions in high regard for their strength, power, and intelligence. But how many of these organizations help the animals that they celebrate in their art? Help call attention to these amazing creatures in art!

NOVICE

MAKING YOUR VOICE HEARD

HOW BIG IS YOUR VOICE? Try to make your voice as loud as possible without any technology. Try a paper cone, or another invention. How loud can you go?

PRACTICE MAKING YOUR VOICE HEARD ON PAPER. Come up with a persuasive argument to save lions—how can you persuade your reader to help them?

RESEARCH LION RESCUE OR CHARITY ORGANIZATIONS THAT HELP LIONS. How do they communicate their message to the world? Do they use social media, newsletters, incentives, or websites? Come up with your own plan to get your message out to the world.

EXTREME

MAPPING LIONS IN YOUR WORLD

EXPLORE YOUR COMMUNITY AND PHOTOGRAPH IMAGES OF LIONS IN LOGOS, SIGNS, STATUES, FLAGS, AND PRODUCTS. You could also get together with an adult and explore the Internet, searching for lions used by companies. If you find it tricky to find any, pick one of the organizations shown on this page.

LIONS AS LOGOS

LIONS OFTEN APPEAR IN LOGOS, SYMBOLS, STATUES, AND CRESTS.
This is because they are seen as symbols of strength, royalty, and intelligence. How many can you find where you live?

GO ONLINE TO CHECK OUT OTHER BUSINESSES THAT INCORPORATE LIONS INTO THEIR LOGO. If it's not clear from their company information, write a letter asking what they do to help lions as part of their business plan.

TAKE UP A LION DONATION. Can you persuade a company that uses a lion in its logo to start giving a regular donation to a lion rescue charity?

KEEP A RECORD of your discoveries by labeling a map and writing notes. Make sure you find out who owns the image of the lion.

ADVOCATE FOR LIONS by writing a letter to the business owner, the town or city government, or whoever owns the lion art. Suggest that they give a regular donation to a lion conservation charity.

>> EXPERT TIPS

Use these tips to be a lion advocate!

1 Advocates are people who speak on behalf of another person or creature. You can be an advocate for lions by learning what they need and sharing with people who can help, like businesses that use lions in their logos.

2 Some businesses have restrictions and you must always be respectful of others' property. If you are not allowed to take photographs, draw a sketch instead.

3 You'll also need to learn how to use maps. The study and creation of maps is called cartography. Make sure to brush up on your map skills online or at your local library so you'll be able to chart where the lions are.

Adult lionesses and cubs rest in the comfort of the pride.

CHAPTER 3

>> LION PRIDE

> "THE MOST COOPERATIVE WE'VE EVER SEEN LIONS IS WHEN IT'S LIFE OR DEATH. IT'S US AGAINST THEM."
>
> —DR. CRAIG PACKER,
> DIRECTOR OF THE LION RESEARCH CENTER

A lion cub perches atop a termite mound in the Okavango Delta in Botswana.

It's not easy to raise a King. Adult lions are ferocious, but lions enter the world as house cats do—small, blind, and helpless. Lion parents feed and protect their cubs for two years, so the cubs can grow strong bones and powerful muscles. That's a long time to be vulnerable in the wild—where predators and other threats loom around every rock and bush.

Other animals will gladly take out future Kings. One less cub means less competition for food and land. And competition in lion territory is fierce—because lions need a lot of land to find enough food all year round.

>> LION SPOTLIGHT
A DAY IN THE LIFE

Lions have a reputation for being lazy—they sleep or lounge in the shade for about 20 hours each day. But really they're storing energy for their next hunt. If you had to stalk and wrestle each of your meals to the ground, you'd sleep a lot, too!

1 hour
eating

2–3 hours
hunting

20 hours
sleeping and lounging

LIONS COUGH UP HAIR BALLS, JUST AS PET CATS DO.

Lions cross through a small stream in Botswana.

Conservationist Dr. Simon Black's tips for studying lions in the field:

1

Be realistic about lions. They are not cuddly pets—quite the opposite.

2

Get used to their sounds, smells, and habits. If you are a bit squeamish about dead animals, try to train yourself to tolerate blood and guts.

3

Get out and about—go trekking, keep fit, and get used to being outside in all weather. Get used to dealing with pesky insects.

LION TERRITORY

For lions, raising successful cubs hinges on one thing: securing the best territory. Prime lion real estate includes plenty of food, water, and shelter. Cubs must eat regularly to survive. Adults need to refuel often, too—it takes a lot of energy to hunt for a family and to fight off invaders. Water hydrates lions, but more importantly, rivers and watering holes make the best year-round hunting grounds.

In Africa's Serengeti National Park, for example, prides that live near areas where two or more rivers merge, called confluences, raise more successful cubs than lions living farther out. During the dry season the sweltering sun evaporates river water, leaving most riverbeds bone dry. River confluences are the only places to find water. Thirsty prey have two choices: die of dehydration, or take their chances at watering holes where lions await them.

But winning the best territory is difficult. Every lion eyes the best land—and they'll risk their lives to fight for it. That's why lions evolved to live in prides—for backup. Larger prides hold their ground more easily. They can also bully other lions out of better territory.

African lion prides typically include four to six related lionesses—mothers, daughters, sisters, aunts, or cousins—along with two or more males, called resident males, and any number of cubs. But prides can be bigger or smaller. The farther you get from the rivers, for example, the less food there is. Prides that live there are often smaller. Africa's largest prides live inside protected parks in East and Southern Africa. Abundant prey keeps these lions well fed, healthy, and multiplying. They form large groups of the biggest, baddest lions on the savanna.

Whatever the pride size, all lions in a pride cooperate to survive.

PROTECTING THEIR TERRITORY

Male lions—with their thick, muscular bodies and short, powerful legs—are built to fight. They often leave the pride for long stretches of the day to patrol their territory. They mark boundary trees and bushes with urine and scratch marks, and they roar loudly to deter invaders. They always keep an eye out for rival prides and hyenas that will kill lion cubs. But the biggest threat to a male lion is a takeover—when marauding males challenge resident males to take control of their territory and their pride.

A takeover threatens the whole pride. The new males immediately kill or chase off all the cubs. Killing a lioness' cubs triggers the females to breed again. This is very important because as soon as the new males take over the clock starts ticking. Resident males typically rule a single pride for only two or three years. It's only a matter of time before the next group of younger, stronger lions comes to challenge them.

While the males deter invaders, female lions secure dinner for the pride. If prey is smaller or scarce—usually during the dry season—lionesses will sometimes pair off and go their separate ways to hunt. Large group hunts are common, too. Lionesses work as a team to bring down prey that is too big or too swift for one or two lions to tackle. But once a kill is made, all bets are off.

Lion prides don't have a strict chain of command, or hierarchy. Once a lion kill hits the ground, it's an all-out brawl of snarling lips and flashing teeth. If the males aren't around, the lionesses fight to secure the best cuts of meat. The only exception to the no-hierarchy rule is that male lions eat what they want when they want. When the females catch dinner, the males muscle their way in and get their fill, leaving the lionesses to battle for the leftovers. Peace returns once mealtime is over.

A CUB IS BORN

Lions are social cats and the only cats that live in prides. They form strong bonds with their pride mates. Lions rub, nuzzle, paw, lick, and cuddle regularly. Female lions bond with other female pride mates, and males bond with the other males—until they're ready to mate.

Resident males regularly sniff under the adult lionesses' tails. A male lion can smell when a female is ready to mate. Resident males will mate with any lioness in the pride. During mating, the male defends the female against other resident males. This guarantees he's the father of her future cubs.

Three and a half months later, the pregnant lioness

LESS THAN HALF OF ALL LION CUBS SURVIVE TO ADULTHOOD.

Milo, one of the last surviving Barbary lion descendants, chows down at his home in the United Kingdom.

MILO THE BARBARY LION

Barbary lions (also known as Atlas lions) once ruled the northern-most tip of Africa—from the snow-peaked Atlas Mountains to the sunny Mediterranean coast. The Sahara desert to the south isolated Barbary lions from other African lions. They evolved distinct features—thickset bodies and long manes extending down their bellies—to cope with a colder, mountainous habitat. Many European and African rulers prized Barbary lions. The Sultans of Morocco kept a collection of them in the Royal Palace gardens at Fez and Rabat. Today, wild Barbary lions are extinct. But researchers recently traced the family tree of around 80 zoo lions back to the Moroccan Royal Collection. Milo is one of those descendants. He lives with his mate Ruti at Port Lympne Wild Animal Park in the U.K. The pair was recently selected to breed in hopes of continuing the Barbary lineage. Only they've hit a snag. Although Milo is in his prime breeding years, he's timid—and Ruti likes to tease him. She lets him near, and then pushes him away. Still, Port Lympne staff hopes to see Ruti sporting a round belly soon!

Curious cubs investigate a camera under the watchful eye of an adult.

LION CLAWS ARE THREE INCHES (8 CM) LONG—ABOUT THE LENGTH OF A HUMAN FINGER!

slips off to a den and gives birth. Newborn cubs weigh about two to four pounds (1 to 2 kg). They have wiry hair and patterned fur. Hidden safely in the den, the cubs drink their mothers' milk for about six weeks. Then they rejoin the pride.

Often, two or more lionesses in a pride give birth at the same time. When this happens, the mothers cluster their cubs into a group, called a crèche, and raise them together—one more advantage of living in a pride. A group of lionesses can defend their cubs from invaders more successfully than a lone lioness can.

The mothers also share hunting and feeding responsibilities. Though they give preference to their own offspring, lionesses will suckle any cubs in their pride.

Well-fed lion cubs have a lot of energy, and they can play for hours at a time. Frisky cubs mimic their parents. They run, stalk, crouch, and pounce on their siblings and cousins for hours each day. They climb uprooted trees and wrestle each other for the highest spot on a bulging rock or towering termite mound. And they practice roaring—though it takes about two years to develop a deep, ferocious roar.

>> **ANIMAL RESCUE!**

LION DETECTIVE

Simon Black didn't intend to be a lion detective. He studied conservation science in college. Then, he began researching Barbary lions—the unique lion subspecies from North Africa, which is now sadly extinct. At least, that's what most people thought. Simon discovered that several Barbary descendants lived in Temara Zoo in Morocco—and others could likely be found in Europe.

Simon contacted and visited several European zoos. He scoured handwritten records to investigate suspected Barbary lions' family histories. Eventually, Simon identified about 80 descendants. He detailed each lion's location, age, gender, and family history. Now, Simon helps zoos arrange healthy breeding pairs. One of the first lions to receive a new mate lives at Olomouc Zoo in the Czech Republic. He is an eight-year-old male also called Simon. He is now paired with a lioness named Lily. The lions bonded, and Lily gave birth to two cubs in 2010. Since then, seven more cubs have been born in other zoos. Thanks to Simon's sleuthing skills, the case of the missing Barbary lions has been solved, and the lions saved from extinction.

I met a seven-year-old boy in Maasailand who had been attacked by a lion when he was only five. The lion wanted to catch the child's goats and batted him out of the way when he tried chasing the lion with his stick. His father was extremely proud of him and showed me his son's scars.

LIONS BEGIN GROWING THEIR MANES AT ABOUT THREE YEARS OLD.

Playful cubs wrestle with their lioness babysitter in the Okavango Delta. Play is an important way that cubs build strength and confidence.

CRAIG PACKER

NAME: CRAIG PACKER
BORN: FORT WORTH, TEXAS
JOB: PROFESSOR AND DIRECTOR, UNIVERSITY OF MINNESOTA'S LION RESEARCH CENTER AND RESEARCH SCIENTIST AT THE TANZANIAN WILDLIFE RESEARCH INSTITUTE
JOB LOCATION: TANZANIA
YEARS WORKING WITH LIONS: 35
MONTHS A YEAR IN THE FIELD: 6

How are you helping to save lions?

My team and I are trying to make it possible for lions to move freely between Ngorongoro Crater and the Serengeti National Park. The Ngorongoro lion population has been isolated so long that it has become very inbred. By helping the local Maasai people improve their livestock husbandry, we hope they will stop killing lions that try to travel between the Crater and the Serengeti. This way, fresh blood can enter the Crater and revitalize the population.

Favorite thing about your job?

Finding out new things—being a scientist is like being an explorer. There's so much still to learn!

Best thing about working in the field?

The excitement of not knowing what you are going to see today. Almost every day is full of surprises.

Worst thing about working in the field?

Worrying about how to find the funding to keep the research program going. Lions are expensive to study!

How can kids prepare to do your job one day?

Do really well in school. Travel a lot—especially to Africa. Be persistent.

It may seem like lion cubs are just messing around, but play is important. Cubs wrestle with their siblings and cousins to build strength. "Play is a way for young ones to learn the moves of a hunt, chase, and kill," says National Geographic Explorer-in-Residence Dereck Joubert. It's how they develop their coordination for when they start to hunt on their own.

Cubs take their first bites of meat at about three months old, tearing small chunks off their mothers' kills. They start going along on hunts a year or so later. Hunting is best learned on the job. A young lion's first few hunting attempts are clumsy. They lose a lot, but each attempt is a valuable lesson. As they grow, they will do better. They must do better, because every lion has to hunt at some point in their lives—even the adult males.

BUILDING A NEW PRIDE

Incoming male lions force young males out of the pride after their third or fourth birthday. Can you imagine being thrown out of your house at three or four years old? But a three-year-old cub is like a teenager in lion years.

Most teenage males team up with their brothers or cousins to form a coalition, and set off together. Single males look for other males to ally with. The more males in a coalition, the better their chances at taking over a pride. Together, young males roam the plains as bachelors until they're strong enough to challenge another pride's resident males.

Females usually join their mothers' prides. But if they are still young at the next takeover, the new males evict teenage females, too. Typically, though, female cubs stay put.

One day, unfamiliar roars will echo through a young lioness's territory. Younger, healthier males will appear and size up her father and the other resident males. The challengers will lunge and grapple with the old guard. Fur will fly. Eventually, the older, exhausted males will back down. The new resident males will mate with the females, and soon the next generation of lions will be born.

LION PLAYGROUND

Lions play and rest on kopjes, termite mounds, and in trees. Termites build large mounds by mixing soil, dung, and their own saliva. A kopje is a small mound or hill made of rock.

Three young male lions stay alert as they rest in each other's company.

SAVING DYLAN

Craig Packer heads the Serengeti Lion Project in Tanzania, Africa. For several months each year, Craig lives and works at the Lion House, his research station in Serengeti National Park. Over 3,000 lions prowl the park. Craig and his team of students navigate the grassland in Land Rovers to study the lions' movements and behaviors. Their research saves lions by informing conservation strategies. But Craig has also saved lions with his bare hands.

Hunters set snare traps throughout the Serengeti to snag bushmeat. One day, Craig spotted a struggling lion lying on the ground. A snare's metal wire clutched the lion's neck. Craig injected the lion with medicine that put it to sleep. Then, Craig and his team freed the lion and cleaned its wounds. They sat with the lion, which they named Dylan, until he woke and could walk on his own. Dylan quickly recovered from the incident—he even took over a pride near the Lion House. The team kept a close eye on him to make sure he didn't get snared again.

>> RESCUE CHALLENGE

NOVICE

GETTING TO KNOW THE FAMILY

Depending on where you live in the world you may have real-life lions prowling your community. For most of us it's more likely that we will see one in a local zoo. Domestic cats are big cats' tiny relatives and can behave in very similar ways. Just watch a little tabby cat stalk through the grass and then pounce on its unsuspecting prey.

This challenge is all about getting to know big cats better by learning to understand their less dangerous and more familiar cousins. Each of these challenges will help you to get into the minds of cats and find ways to study them in the field.

PICK A CAT AND FOLLOW IT AROUND. Introduce it to different rooms in the house or habitats outdoors (if it's an outdoor cat). Does it behave differently when in a different place?

TRY MIRRORING ITS BEHAVIOR. Can you communicate with it? Record poses and communication efforts in a notebook.

ANALYZE YOUR FINDINGS. Which of your cat's behaviors are most like a lion's? Can you start to think like a cat? Can you start to think like a big cat?

EXTREME

CARRY OUT A LOCAL EXPEDITION with friends and family and complete a survey of all the cats in your neighborhood.

ADVANCED

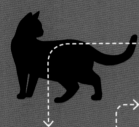

PHOTOGRAPH any domestic cats that look the most and least like lions. You can also try filming what your cat sees from its eye level.

Make sure to capture them in **DIFFERENT POSES**, stalking, grooming, walking, or running.

→ Print your images and lay them out on a table and **CATEGORIZE THEM** according to pose, behavior, and look. Cut out or print photos of lions, too.

→ Get a piece of poster board and **CREATE A COOL CAT COLLAGE** to hang in your room or locker, or make a journal, scrapbook, or other keepsake. And check out your cool video!

>> **EXPERT TIPS**

You will need to start to think and act like a cat to do this challenge successfully.

1 Take care that you are very careful when doing this challenge. Even small cats are equipped with teeth and claws that can hurt you. Arched backs, hissing, and teeth displays are all good reasons to keep your distance.

2 Be curious, explore your house at night, nap during the day, lick your hands, grow claws, purr when you like things, pounce, and try balancing on things. That's the way of a cat!

3 Learn to move like a cat, mirroring their behaviors. Can you convince a cat that you are one, too?

A CAT'S HEART BEATS TWICE AS FAST AS A HUMAN'S.

Each member should **KEEP A PHOTOGRAPHIC RECORD** of each cat along with notes on where you have spotted it, any markings, its name, behaviors, and routes it takes.

→ Buy, print, or **MAKE A MAP OF YOUR SURVEY AREA.** Make sure you label and code your map with your findings like each cat's territory, routes, and other cats it might run into!

61

CHAPTER 4
> ON THE PROWL

"I AM **NOT AFRAID** OF AN ARMY OF LIONS LED BY A SHEEP; I AM **AFRAID** OF AN ARMY OF SHEEP LED BY A LION."

— ALEXANDER THE GREAT

Buffalo, wildebeest, and zebras tense. Their eyes survey the horizon for lions. A slight ruffle in the knee-high grass signals a zebra herd to run. Dust kicks up at their feet, and the calm turns to chaos.

Lions thrive in chaos. It makes hunting easier. Two lionesses quickly zero in on a limping adult. The zebra is injured—a perfect mark for hungry lions. They bee-line toward the straggler.

One lioness swats the zebra's hind legs with her large paws, tripping the animal. The second lioness launches from her hind legs and wraps her muscular forelegs around the zebra's neck. The zebra drops to the ground.

BORN TO KILL

Hunting is what lions do best. Their physical weapons—including powerful legs; knife-like claws; and meat-shredding, bone-crunching teeth—give lions an edge over their prey.

But to be successful, lions must also outsmart their prey, always staying one step ahead. Lions memorize every inch of their territories. They store detailed, 3-D maps in their brains, like in a video game. They know the location of every prey's favorite rest sites, watering holes, and worn paths. Lions easily recall the best lookout points in their territory and the best spots to launch an ambush.

Like silent ninjas, lions are masters of the stealth approach. Their padded feet make barely a sound on soft grass and sand. And their tan-colored coats blend into their natural habitat. A lion's prey almost never sees it coming—until it's too late. Lions use two main

> **LIONS OFTEN FOLLOW CIRCLING VULTURES TO A FRESH KILL—AND TRY TO STEAL A MEAL FROM THE PREDATOR WHO KILLED IT.**

PROTECTING ASIATIC LIONS

On an early winter morning in Junagadh, India, Kausik Banerjee receives a call: two lionesses have been spotted in a sugarcane field about 15 miles (24 km) outside the Girnar Sanctuary. One of them wears a radio collar around its neck. Can he help? Kausik grabs his GPS tracking device, jumps in his jeep, and drives toward the field. He quickly narrows in on the lionesses, and approaches them cautiously. The lionesses turn back toward the sanctuary, but Kausik follows them to ensure a safe return. Finally, after five long hours, the lionesses slip back into the Girnar Sanctuary.

Kausik is a senior research fellow at the Wildlife Institute of India (WII). He records Asiatic lions' movements in and around Gir Forest to determine important lion habitats. Thanks to Kausik and his colleagues' work at WII, the government designated a patch of land between Gir Forest and Girnar Sanctuary an Eco-sensitive Zone. This curbs land development there, so the lions can continue to move freely between the two forests. Kausik and his colleagues are now mapping other areas that need protection, so that the Asiatic lion population can continue to grow.

Two Asiatic lions and their cubs find shelter in the Gir Forest in India. The average pride size in the dense Gir Forest is two females, two males, and their cubs.

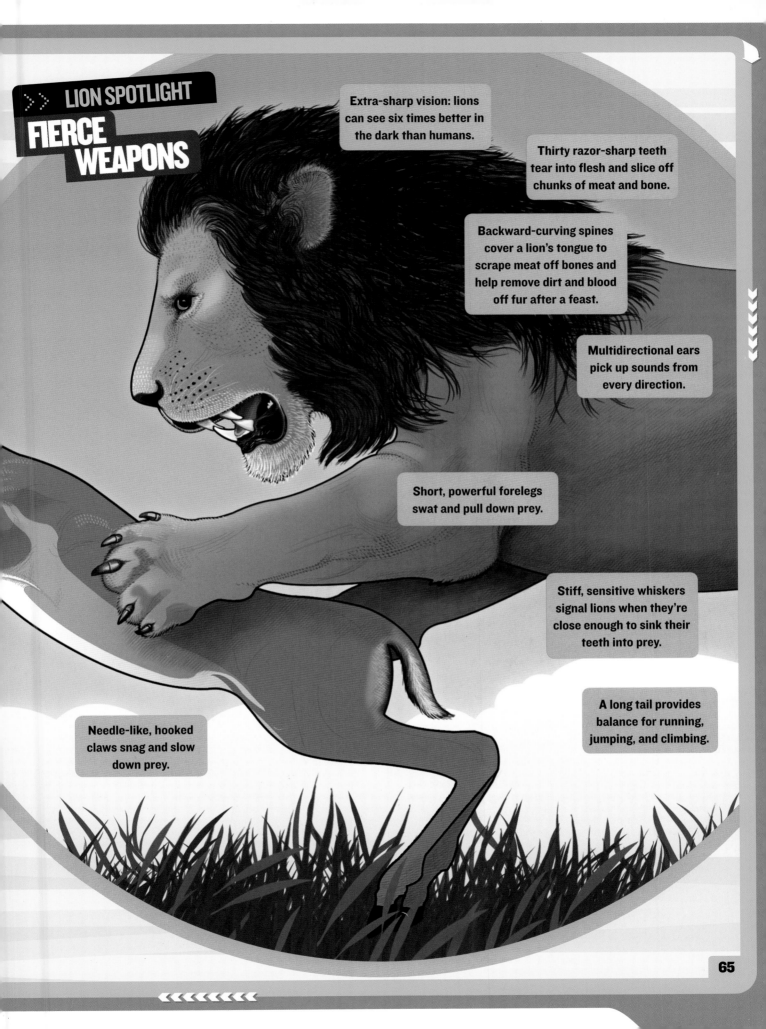

hunting strategies that they fine-tune for different prey species.

The "search and stalk" method is a favorite among lions living in open plains. Lions set out on a long search, checking every reliable prey path and rest stop on their list. When they eye prey ahead, they freeze—like a house cat stalking catnip. Then, they silently advance. Once within striking distance, they charge.

The lions' second go-to strategy— the "sit and wait"—requires more patience. In this scenario, lions arrive at a rest site long before their prey. Each lion picks its hiding spot—and they settle in. It could be hours before a zebra or antelope shows up. But as soon as the prey animals relax, the lions pounce!

ONE HUNGRY CAT

In lion territory, no animal is safe. Lions are opportunistic hunters, meaning they will eat any animal around if they're hungry enough. They'll eat everything from birds (including ostriches) to whale carcasses washed up on African beaches. The only animal not normally on lions' menu are adult elephants (because they're so big and powerful)—unless the elephant is sick, injured, or walking around by itself. Then, it's fair game.

Lion prey varies by geography and season. Savanna Africa endures extreme wet and dry seasons. In the wet season, herds of buffalo, zebra, wildebeest, and impala are plentiful. Soon the rains dry up and the grass is reduced to mere nubs. Only the hardiest warthogs and gazelles remain. Lions prefer medium-size ungulates, or hoofed animals: wildebeest, impala, zebra, gazelles, and buffalo. In their absence, the lions adapt.

Lions can hunt alone, and they do. A female lioness is powerful enough to kill a warthog or wildebeest on her own. But group hunting improves a lion's chance of success against larger prey. Group hunts are carefully orchestrated events. For example, each lioness in one pride at Etosha National Park in Namibia takes on a specific role. Some lions act as "wings" by fanning out and circling prey on long stalks. The "center" position carefully stays put until the wings drive the prey their way. Then they attack.

LIGERS AREN'T THE ONLY KIND OF HYBRID. OFFSPRING OF A MALE TIGER AND A FEMALE LION ARE CALLED TIGONS.

HERCULES THE LION

Meet Hercules, a 900-pound (408-kg), 12-foot (3.7-m)-long behemoth feline. Like Hercules the mythological hero—whose mother is a mortal and father is a Greek god—Hercules the cat is also a mixed breed. He's a liger, meaning his father is a lion and his mother is a tiger. A liger isn't a separate species. It's a rare, big cat hybrid that occurs only in captivity. And like mythological heroes, ligers inherit unique traits from both parents—some positive, some negative.

Adult ligers have tan fur, like lions, with faint tiger stripes—and they're enormous. Ligers lack a growth-inhibiting gene; all their features are supersized. So are their appetites. Hercules eats about 25 pounds (11 kg) of raw meat per day! Though these colossal cats look cool, they're not natural. Lion and tiger offspring are vulnerable to glitches that can cause severe health problems, such as organ failure. That's why most scientists and big cat advocates think these feline hybrids are a bad idea.

Lion prides develop many attack strategies. Once lions solve the riddle of how to hunt a specific prey species, they become specialists. For example, most lions hate water. They'll dip their paws into a small puddle and wince. But on Duba Island, in Botswana's Okavango Delta, the Tsaro Pride—led by the lioness the Jouberts followed in their film *The Last Lions,* Ma di Tau—takes advantage of water.

Hunting powerful Cape buffalo is difficult, even for

TO THE TREETOPS!

Lions climb trees to get a clearer view of their territory, to avoid soggy ground in wet weather, and to escape from stampeding buffalo or swarms of biting flies!

Three lionesses overtake a buffalo in the Okavango Delta in Botswana.

a group of skilled huntresses. But the Tsaro Pride learned to ambush the buffalo in water. The herd panics and scatters when the lions charge, making it easier for the lions to snag slower herd members.

In nearby Chobe National Park, one lion pride stalks elephants at night. Lions have a reflective layer of cells at the back of their eyes. Light from the stars or the moon hits the cells and bounces forward, like a car's headlights. Animals and surroundings appear brighter than they are. The Chobe lions follow the elephant herd at night and mostly attack wounded or lone individuals, including large bulls that fall back.

Lions have no limit to how they adapt their hunting strategies. Though lionesses do most of the hunting for a pride, male lions will go on solo ambush hunts if there's enough thick foliage or dense brush to hide their showy manes. Males will also step in to help lionesses bring down large prey.

A lioness splashes through floodwaters of the Okavango Delta as she charges her prey.

>> EXPERT TIPS

Lion researcher Kausik Banerjee's tips for learning about lions:

1 Be prepared to go to Africa or India if you want to study wild lions.

2 If you cannot get to either of these places, try out a wildlife or environmental class at school or volunteer at a zoo.

3 Be a "Lion-Heart": brave and bold but generous.

FIERCE PREDATORS

The Mountain Pride at Kruger National Park in South Africa employed a total team effort on one hunt. It started with the lionesses' exhaustive search and stalk: Six lionesses follow an adult male giraffe undetected to a dense patch of forest. They crouch low and silent in the grass. The lions eye the giraffe as he snags and chomps acacia leaves. They watch him stumble over the rocky terrain. Giraffes can usually outrun lions, but the rocks here will make escape more difficult. The lionesses settle in and wait patiently.

Night falls, and the lionesses creep into formation. They encircle the towering giraffe—the tops of their heads barely reach his kneecaps. Then, the giraffe spots the lions and launches an offensive attack. He throws powerful blows with his hind legs that could badly injure or kill a lion. The lionesses twist their flexible, 400-pound (181-kg) frames in midair, like small house cats falling from a tree or tall porch. They gracefully dodge the giraffe's blows and take turns leaping onto his hind legs. One after another, the lionesses relentlessly challenge the giraffe.

Finally, fatigue sets in and the lionesses withdraw. Just then reinforcement arrives. The pride's male lions

A lion pride feeds on a young elephant in Zakouma National Park in Chad.

approach and relieve the tired lionesses. With fresh bodies and untapped energy, the males lunge at the giraffe. Now, completely exhausted, the giraffe collapses under the lions' weight.

It was a close call for the lions. They drained their energy and nearly lost their meal. But the truth is lions often lose more than they win. Armed with

ANIMAL SUPERPOWERS

POWER SNIFFERS

LIONS CAN SMELL 30 TIMES BETTER THAN HUMANS — THANKS TO A SPECIAL SCENT ORGAN IN THEIR NOSE.

30x

AND THEY TWIST THEIR FACE IN A FUNNY WAY TO ACCESS IT.

FIRST, A LION OPENS ITS MOUTH. THEN, IT LIFTS ITS CHIN AND WRINKLES ITS NOSE TO "DRINK IN" THE SCENT.

LIONS MOSTLY USE THIS SUPERPOWER TO SNIFF URINE-SPLASHED TREES OR ROCKS TO DETERMINE WHETHER OTHER LIONS ARE PRESENT.

A lion claims the remains of a fallen giraffe following a hunt in the Hanib riverbed of Skeleton Coast Park in western Namibia.

LIONS EAT ABOUT 18 POUNDS (8 KG) OF MEAT PER DAY—THAT WOULD BE LIKE A HUMAN EATING MORE THAN 70 HAMBURGERS!

THANDIWE MWEETWA

Thandiwe ("Thandi") Mweetwa started learning about lions as a young girl—and never stopped. The wild animals she saw on TV sparked her interest. They looked nothing like the small birds and insects she saw in Mazabuka, the town in southern Zambia where she lived. Her mother fueled Thandi's curiosity with stories about lions that prowled the Luangwa Valley in eastern Zambia, where Thandi's mother grew up. When Thandi was 12 years old, she moved with her parents back to the valley of her mother's youth.

In her new village, elephants roved through her backyard. Hippos swam and eagles fished in the lake she passed on her way to school. Monkeys even snuck into her house to look for food! Thandi loved seeing animals in their natural habitat. She joined her school's conservation club and she studied hard in class. Eventually, Thandi turned her passion into a career.

Thandi earned a scholarship to college and studied biology. During the summers, she flew home to Zambia to work for the Zambian Carnivore Programme. Now, Thandi not only studies lions, she teaches others why it's important to conserve them, and how. She rejoined her old school's conservation club as an educator. Lately she's been teaching the children how scientists study wildlife. First, they observe the animals in their habitat. They then ask and answer questions about what they see. It excites her to hear the children talk about how they will apply this knowledge to other school projects.

But for Thandi, this is only the beginning. She's back in school studying for her master's degree. She plans to work with lions—and people—for as long as she can, with one goal in mind: to inspire future generations of children to take action.

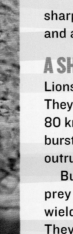

sharp teeth, heavy hooves, and dagger-like horns and antlers, lion prey fight back. Or they flee.

A SHOW OF STRENGTH

Lions are built for short bursts of speed and power. They can accelerate from 0 to 50 miles an hour (0 to 80 km/h) in the blink of an eye. But only in short bursts. If their target gets a head start, it can often outrun lions. This means timing is key.

Buffalo cause more lion deaths than any other prey species. Adult buffalo can weigh over a ton and wield five-foot (1.5-m)-long horns on their heads. They lower their heads and swipe viciously at incoming lions. Buffalo don't give up easily—and they are fiercely protective of their herd. A fleeing buffalo herd will thunder back toward the distress cry of a single member. They charge at lions,

A lioness dodges the sharp, heavy horns of a Cape buffalo.

Spotted hyenas chase away a lion, their main competition, on the plains of the Maasai Mara National Reserve in Kenya.

warning them off with their horns. Sometimes the buffalo win, and the lions fall back. But they can be sure the lions will return.

Successful lions must eat quickly. Scavengers lurk around every corner—especially hyenas and wild dogs. Hyenas are fearsome killers in their own right, but it's often easier to steal someone else's hard-won meal. One-on-one, a lion will always win a skirmish with a hyena. But if hyenas heavily outnumber lions, the lions will accept defeat and move on.

In the wild, lions work for every meal, often risking injury and death. Not everyone can make it to the next generation. The survivors carry on.

ONCE A LION'S BELLY IS FULL, IT CAN SURVIVE FOR MORE THAN A WEEK WITHOUT EATING.

>> RESCUE CHALLENGE

NOVICE

MARK YOUR TERRITORY

Cats are territorial animals. Like you, they like to have their own space. If another lion enters their territory, they'll try to fight them off. For a male lion, losing his territory can mean losing his pride.

Lions mark their territories in a number of different ways. Poop, pee, and glandular secretions can all be used to mark the borders between lion territories. Lions will also leave scratch marks on trees to warn others to stay away. This challenge is all about marking out your territory.

PROTECTING TERRITORY

CREATE YOUR OWN GAME that involves protecting a territory. Try a game of capture the flag, build a board game, or make up a totally new game! Involve lions as characters in your game.

If you're outside, **USE MUD TO MAKE SCRATCH MARKS** on trees to mark the borders of your game. Patrol your borders—you want to protect what's yours!

KEEP SCORE and observe what territories different friends pick out. What are their advantages? Disadvantages?

EXTREME

SPRAY LIKE A LION!

EVERY LION'S SPRAY SMELLS A LITTLE DIFFERENT. Mix together your own spray using water and smelly edible things you can find in your kitchen.

Once you've finished, **USE A WATER PISTOL** or perfume bottle to **SPRAY IT ON THE EDGES OF YOUR TERRITORY.** Can your friends find your smell?

LIONS ALSO USE THEIR SPRAY AS A SIGN OF AFFECTION by rubbing it on their friends or mates. You could too—but make sure to ask first!

Lion spray can be very smelly. It needs to be so that other cats can find it. When doing this challenge:

1

Only use ingredients that will not lead to lots of waste, and don't include anything hot, poisonous, or dangerous.

2

Use smells that will make your spray distinctive. Ideal scents include: mint, vanilla, chocolate, orange, and lemon.

3

For the ultimate sniff test, try spraying on a piece of thin paper and letting it dry. Can you still smell your scent?

ADVANCED

ROAMING LIKE A LION

1. Roam like a lion by hiking eight miles (12.9 km). This would be only one side of a small lion range.

2. Observe what you encounter on your hike. Do you hear airplanes? Pass by farms or houses? How many people do you see? Imagine what this might be like for a wild lion.

3. Check out the natural landscape or formations that might be useful for a lion pride. Is there a place to safely raise cubs? Lots of potential prey? A nearby water source?

4. Take pictures along your route and print out or cut out pictures of lions to paste in the scene. Now there are lions in your backyard!

TRADE SCENTS WITH YOUR FRIENDS. What do theirs smell like, and how are they different from yours? **HAVE A SNIFF CONTEST** by competing to see who can identify the most scents.

"AS WE DE-LINK OURSELVES SPIRITUALLY FROM THESE ANIMALS, WE LOSE HOPE, WE LOSE THAT THING WITHIN US THAT KEEPS US CONNECTED TO THE PLANET."

—DERECK JOUBERT, NATIONAL GEOGRAPHIC EXPLORER-IN-RESIDENCE

CHAPTER 5

>> LIONS AND PEOPLE

Prehistoric art expert Jean Clottes inspects ancient charcoal paintings discovered deep underground at Chauvet Cave in southern France.

The human-lion relationship is complicated. Through the centuries, humans have respected lions. Ancient human cultures worshipped lion-like gods and goddesses. And people have killed lions. This tug-of-war relationship has deep, tangled roots that date back thousands of years.

DECEMBER 18, 1994

It's a cold December day in southern France's Ardèche Valley when cave explorer Jean-Marie Chauvet and two friends make a startling discovery. It starts off as an ordinary day in a small limestone cave. Other people have been to this spot before, but Jean-Marie received a tip from another explorer that something more might be hidden inside. He leads his friends to the end of the cave. There, an air current blows through a small opening in a pile of stones. Where is

>> ANIMAL RESCUE!

LION ZOOKEEPER

Rebecca Kregar Stites fell in love with African lions after coming face to face with the big cats on a trip to Kruger National Park in South Africa. Now, Rebecca works with lions every day—not in the wild, but in Washington, D.C., at the Smithsonian Institution's National Zoo. As an animal keeper there, Rebecca helps maintain a healthy zoo lion population that conservationists could someday reintroduce into the wild—if wild lions become extinct. Since all lions have wild instincts no matter where they live, Rebecca uses a few tricks that make the lions' checkups safe and easy.

Rebecca trains the lions to respond to hand signals. One signal prompts the lions to approach the edge of their enclosure and open their mouths, as if to say "ah." Then Rebecca can look for chipped or cracked teeth. She also trains the lions to lie down and present their backsides or tails next to the chain-link wall, so the veterinarians can inject them with vaccines or draw blood. How do you get a lion to volunteer for an injection? Rebecca rewards them during training with their favorite snack—raw meatballs. Keeping zoo lions healthy is critical, but reintroducing large carnivores into the wild is difficult. So Rebecca's most important job is to educate zoo visitors about the threats wild lions face. She hopes this information will inspire others to take action and help save wild lions before they disappear.

MALE LIONS TYPICALLY SURVIVE NO LONGER THAN 12 YEARS IN THE WILD. FEMALES AVERAGE 13 TO 15 YEARS. ZOO LIONS CAN SURVIVE UP TO 30 YEARS.

ANCIENT LION HEROES

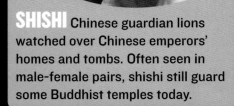

SHISHI Chinese guardian lions watched over Chinese emperors' homes and tombs. Often seen in male-female pairs, shishi still guard some Buddhist temples today.

SEKHMET (aka Powerful One) Ancient Egyptians worshipped this lion-headed goddess. Sekhmet protected pharaohs in battle. She cast plagues on enemies, but she could also protect people from the plague and cure diseases.

NARASIMHA (aka Man-Lion) Narasimha is the ancient Hindu god Vishnu's lion-like avatar. Vishnu transformed into Narasimha to kill the invincible demon Hiranyakashipu.

APEDEMAC Ancient Nubians worshipped this lion-headed war god. Apedemac helped Nubian pharaohs defeat enemies and win wars.

the air coming from? *The hole must lead to another room—a secret cave.*

One by one they remove the stones. They squeeze through the narrow passage and start down a dusty path. Soon the cave floor drops into a deep shaft.

The explorers descend. They spot red marks on a stalactite and stop dead in their tracks. There, hidden in the darkness, is a detailed painting of a mammoth. Every step the explorers take reveals more paintings and charcoal drawings on the cave walls—horses, bison, reindeer . . . and lions. Lots of very detailed lions. But these drawings were not made recently—they're Stone Age drawings. The humans that sketched these lions lived in this cave more than 30,000 years ago.

The exact relationship between Stone Age humans and lions is unclear. But the Chauvet Cave drawings hint that humans knew lions intimately. They drew whisker marks on the lions' muzzles—a detail someone could learn only by studying lions up close.

SYMBOLS OF THE ANCIENTS

But these paintings aren't the first ancient clue. The "Lion Man" is a small ivory figure carved from a mammoth tusk. It's about 35,000 years old. Archaeologists pieced it together from hundreds of fragments unearthed in a cave in the German Alps. Lion Man has a lion head and upper body, but human legs and feet. What could this mean? Some scientists think Lion Man represents a spiritual connection between Stone Age humans and lions. We can't be certain, but we do know that other ancient cultures considered lions sacred.

Ancient Egyptians, for example, worshipped half-lion-half-human gods more than 3,000 years ago. Egyptian kings, called pharaohs, also raised lion cubs as pets. Lions sat near the pharaohs' thrones and ran alongside their chariots. They stood guard over important temples. People even mummified lions when they died.

Ancient Egyptians built stone monuments to honor lions, too. A colossal stone sphinx—a creature that

>> LION PROFILE
LEO (& YOU)

If you celebrate your birthday on or between July 23 and August 22, you are a lion. At least, you're a lion in the eyes of ancient astrologers. Ancient cultures studied stars, the sun, and the moon—like scientists do today, only they didn't have fancy equipment. But they mapped the stars and decoded their secrets. People used star maps to create calendars, determine the best days to plant crops, and guide them to distant lands. People also named stars and star clusters, or constellations.

Leo—which means lion in Greek—is the name of one popular star cluster. Ancient astrologers thought that if you draw an imaginary line between the stars in constellation Leo and "connect the dots," it looks like the outline of a lion. They linked the constellation to the dates above. People born on those days are said to have lion-like qualities: bravery, strength, loyalty, and pride. Are you a lion?

has a king's head and a lion's body—sits in front of an ancient Egyptian temple. It's one of the largest stone statues in the world.

Lions graced other ancient kingdoms, too. A pride of lions made from gold guarded King Solomon of Israel's throne. Single lions sat beneath the armrests. Assyrian kings from Mesopotamia hunted lions and captured their cubs to keep as pets.

People's fascination with lions continued into the Middle Ages. Kings and emperors kept exotic animals in private collections, called menageries. And they gave lions as gifts to other rulers. The Holy Roman Emperor Frederick II famously gave King Henry III of England three lions for his royal menagerie. And King Louis XV had a large menagerie that included lions at the Palace of Versailles. Curious people traveled to palaces to view the animals up close—much like people visit zoos today.

LIONS TODAY

We still erect massive lion statues to guard our cities, parks, and libraries. Two marble lions nicknamed Patience and Fortitude guard the New York Public Library in the U.S. Since their debut in 1911, Patience and Fortitude have been photographed by tourists, illustrated in children's books, and even appeared in a Hollywood film. Other popular films like *The Lion King* and *Madagascar* portray lovable lion characters. We name countless sports teams after lions. And the royal connection is still strong in England: Lions flank Queen Elizabeth II's family crest.

But for as much as people have respected lions, we kill them relentlessly. Ancient cultures hunted lions, and we continue to hunt them today.

SPORT HUNTING

Sport hunting is a big business in Africa. Hunters travel there from countries all over the world and pay thousands of dollars to shoot a single lion. They ship the lion's stuffed head and body back home to display as trophies. Lion claws, skins, skulls, and whole bodies are also shipped overseas for sale in international markets. More than half of these lion exports

THE BRIGHTEST STAR IN THE LEO CONSTELLATION IS CALLED REGULUS, WHICH MEANS "LITTLE KING."

With a little imagination, the stars in the night sky become Leo the lion.

A row of stone sphinxes lines the Avenue of Sphinxes in Luxor, Egypt. Ancient Egyptians built this sacred road to connect the great temples along the Nile River more than 2,000 years ago.

and hunting trophies end up in the United States.

Sport hunting *is* legal—even inside some national parks—as long as people buy the appropriate licenses. But many hunting operations are poorly managed. People are killing lions faster than lions can multiply. Illegal hunting makes the problem worse. It happens all over Africa, and it's taking a toll on lion populations.

LIONS IN TRADITION

Some African warrior tribes—like the Maasai in southern Kenya and northern Tanzania—kill lions to prove their bravery. As part of their warrior initiation, young male Maasai stalk, wrestle, and spear a male lion. They harvest the lion's mane, tail, and claws to keep as trophies.

This ritual, called *olamayio,* is important to Maasai culture. It earns young warriors respect in their communities—even more than a college degree or a good-paying job.

A skilled spearman called a venator confronts a lion in a Roman fresco, or painting.

>> EXPLORER PROFILE

BEVERLY & DERECK JOUBERT

BORN: SOUTH AFRICA
JOB TITLE: NATIONAL GEOGRAPHIC EXPLORERS-IN-RESIDENCE
AFFILIATIONS: NATIONAL GEOGRAPHIC SOCIETY, WILDLIFE FILMS BOTSWANA, GREAT PLAINS CONSERVATION, AND SEVERAL OTHER ORGANIZATIONS
JOB LOCATION: DUBA PLAINS, BOTSWANA; JOHANNESBURG, SOUTH AFRICA; AND MARA PLAINS AND MAASAILAND, KENYA
YEARS WORKING WITH LIONS: ABOUT 30
MONTHS A YEAR IN THE FIELD: 6-11

How are you helping to save lions?

We work on the ground with various levels of anti-poaching, anti-smuggling efforts in Botswana and in Kenya. We work with governments at the highest level in three countries trying to change policy for managing lions. We started the Big Cats Initiative with National Geographic because we felt that even as Explorers-in-Residence we weren't making enough of a difference. With other organizations we have created political cases to ban lion hunting and to list lions as endangered.

Favorite thing about your job?

We enjoy setting out at 4 a.m. when the stars are still glowing in a way they only glow in Africa, bright and clear and before the sun comes up, and then finding lions moving through the mist at dawn, hunting buffalo.

Best thing about working in the field?

The lack of clutter, the skies are clear, there is no TV, no noise, no cell phones calling you, and this allows us to focus 100 percent on what we do.

Worst thing about working in the field?

None. Okay . . . the worst is finally packing our small plane and heading to town for a long edit or a series of talks around the world and leaving behind the stories, the lives of the cats we have been following, and knowing we will be missing out.

How can kids prepare to do your job one day?

Filming and conservation is not just about science. Science can tell you how things work but not why. And more and more we need to know why. Do the science degree, but understand, don't just learn. Have a passion, don't just be rational. Anyone who can bridge science and art, or science and conservation philosophy will lead us into the future where we all need solutions.

Many, a lioness we had followed for years, was introducing her two-week-old cubs to the pride for the first time. It was tense. The pride could easily attack and kill them. She was growling and unhappy. The pride was on a kill. But she came up to us and left the cubs at our feet (our vehicle has no doors), and after a very steady sniff of my leg, she trusted us to protect the cubs while she went about calming the pride down.

The Jouberts film and photograph a group of lions at mealtime while working in the field.

>> **ANIMAL RESCUE!**

PROTECTING LIONS FROM POACHERS

Snare poaching is rampant in Zambia's Luangwa Valley—a vast area that spans several national parks and holds the country's largest lion population. Matt Becker heads the Zambian Carnivore Programme (ZCP) there. After freeing several lions from deadly snares, everyone in ZCP decided they needed to do more. They teamed with the South Luangwa Conservation Society (SLCS) to map the highest-risk snare areas, and they deployed a Lion Anti-Snaring Team to patrol them. In less than two years, the team removed 357 snares from their study area and rescued four snared lions.

The rescued lions—which included two males and two females—fully recovered and have since produced 35 cubs! By saving four snared lions, the team actually saved 39 lions . . . and counting, plus countless antelope and other lion prey that would have been caught in the snares. But snaring in the Luangwa Valley is on the rise. As the team continues to destroy snares, they also work with Zambian policy-makers to develop policies that will hopefully stamp out snaring in the area for good. Check out the ZCP at zambiacarnivores.org.

The anti-snare team works to remove snares that could kill or injure lions.

One Maasai warrior, called Sainepune, has killed several lions over the years. And he has no plans to stop. "I grew up when there was no conservation, and lions were being killed. They are still here," he says. "We have inherited lion hunting as a tradition."

Traditions involving lions are common in Africa. Some African tribes—especially in parts of western and south-eastern Africa—eat lion meat and make medicine from lion body parts. They believe this medicine can heal broken bones, back pain, and other ailments. People either hunt the lions themselves—without buying licenses—or they buy body parts from lion poachers.

LION POACHING

Poaching of all kinds harms lions, even when lions aren't the direct targets. Poachers hunt and trap many animal species—from chimpanzees to elephants. They illegally sell the meat—called bushmeat—at local markets and in African cities.

It's hard to quantify illegal activities, because the people responsible are secretive. But officials at France's Roissy-Charles de Gaulle Airport—a large international airport—recently busted several passengers transporting bushmeat in their suitcases. Airport

Rows of rifles point toward a large photo of a lion hanging on the wall at the National Firearms Museum in Fairfax, Virginia, U.S.A.

IN AFRICA TODAY, THERE ARE ONLY 67 KNOWN AREAS WHERE LIONS LIVE.

A clan of spotted hyenas approaches a lion kill in Chobe National Park in Botswana.

DEADLY LEFTOVERS!

Lots of animals scavenge lion kills, making them vulnerable to poison-laced carcass traps:

Jackal

Cheetah

Leopard

Hyena

Wild Dog

Eagle

Vulture

officials estimate that more than 10,000 pounds (4,535 kg) of bushmeat illegally passes through their gates every *week*. Other experts estimate that the worldwide bushmeat trade is worth around one billion dollars a year.

The bushmeat trade has caused severe declines—even extinctions—in local lion populations in national parks throughout Africa. Poaching is especially bad in West and Central Africa.

Comoé National Park in Ivory Coast is one of the largest protected areas in West Africa. About the size of the U.S. state of Connecticut, the park is lined with savannas, woodlands, forests, and the gushing Comoé River. Prime lion real estate. But researchers combing the area on foot found no traces of lions—though they did encounter many farmers grazing their cattle inside the parks and several poaching campsites.

Michelle Kastern tracks radio-collared lions in Africa.

MICHELLE KASTERN

The Kavango Zambezi Transfrontier Conservation Area (KAZA) is a new peace park in southern Africa. Spanning five countries, it is a wildlife sanctuary that aims to promote ecotourism and is now the largest peace park in the world. But only if it succeeds.

Michelle Kastern is doing her part to make sure it does. Many areas of the park have high human-wildlife conflict. The East Caprivi section in Namibia is one of them. As part of her graduate course work at Stellenbosch University in South Africa, Michelle radio-collars lions there, mapping their every move.

Michelle uses the lion maps in two ways. People in East Caprivi lose a lot of cattle to lions. By tracking the lions, Michelle is able to warn local villagers when lions are near. That way they can corral their cattle in protective enclosures.

One time, a lion pride that had already taken 15 cattle from the area was back on the prowl. This time, Michelle sounded the alarm. Local park rangers patrolled the area, and the farmers watched their cattle closely. The lions were unsuccessful on their hunt.

But the farmers know the lions will be back. That's why Michelle also shares her data with KAZA park officials. They use the maps and other information to identify areas in the park with the most lion traffic. They try to reduce conflict between humans and lions there first. Michelle hopes East Caprivi will be one of those areas. It would help the local people and bring the peace park one step closer to success.

Surveys in Congo, Ghana, and the Democratic Republic of Congo returned similar results. Lions that do still exist in these countries likely live in small, isolated groups. Surprisingly, the researchers found lions in only one country they surveyed: Nigeria. But with fewer than 50 lions remaining in two separate areas their outlook is grim.

Small, isolated lion populations inbreed. Soon, the animals' genes start to look the same. Animals with low genetic diversity become more vulnerable to disease. And as humans inch closer and closer to lion territory, they—along with their pets and their livestock—introduce diseases the lions aren't used to.

Back in Africa, in 1994, a disease carried by domestic dogs—called canine distemper virus—spread like wildfire through Tanzania's Serengeti ecosystem and into neighboring parks. One thousand lions died.

As people continue to march farther into lion territory, more lions will face the same fate. And there's no sign of retreat. Africa and Asia have the two fastest growing human populations in the world. And it's a stone cold fact: As human numbers increase, lion numbers decrease. Unless we take action now, the animals we once considered sacred could vanish from the wild for good.

USE YOUR POWER

There is a saying that "the pen is mightier than the sword." You have the power to share your opinions, and encourage people to help protect big cats.

Everything is connected, including lions and you. You may have directly "met" a living lion in a zoo, in the wild, or seen one in a museum. If not, your links to lions may be less obvious, though still there. You may know someone who has gotten close to, photographed, or even shot one. Maybe your government allows imports of lion parts, or you have bought food from a company that has grown crops on what used to be lion territory. You have certainly read about what National Geographic explorers and conservationists do to help lions. You are doing this right now, and that connects us. Try brainstorming as many of your connections to lions as you can.

In this challenge you will choose, write, share, and send words that will directly connect you to people who influence lions' lives. By sending your opinions to these people, you will be helping to save lions.

NOVICE

ADOPT, DONATE, PETITION

WRITE YOUR NAME ON A PETITION that helps to save lions. There are many great causes all over the world. Some include National Geographic's Big Cats Initiative, the World Wildlife Fund, and LionAid.
You can also **ADOPT A LION** through a charity or other organization. Develop a unique and interactive program to raise money from friends, teachers, and neighbors to adopt a lion. You could also **DEVELOP A FUND-RAISING PROGRAM** to donate to organizations that help lions. National Geographic's Big Cats Initiative has text donations, or kids can dress like a big cat on Halloween and collect coins for big cats. Gather your friends and family to help. Many other organizations also have really cool ways to raise money.

EXTREME

CAUSE AN UPROAR

CREATE A MESSAGE TO BE SENT TO AN INDIVIDUAL OR ORGANIZATION that could be doing more to help lions. Individuals could include celebrities, influential people in media, or CEOs of large companies.

You could pick an organization that is directly killing lions or causing habitat loss. You could send your message just from you, but your words will be even more powerful if you persuade other people to

WRITE LETTERS TO LIONS

Filmmakers and National Geographic Explorers-in-Residence DERECK AND BEVERLY JOUBERT want you to HELP SAVE LIONS! Write letters to lions, and the Jouberts will deliver them to African leaders to let them know how important lions are to kids everywhere.

DRAW A PICTURE OF A LION TO GO WITH YOUR LETTER. Use what you've learned about size, features, and endangered status to influence your image. Visit kids.nationalgeographic.com/kids/activities/letters-to-lions to find out how you can help.

support you. A great way to do this is by creating a petition that you can put in the mail. Showing that you're supported by 100, 1,000, or even more people will amplify your message!

Use these tips to help create your own powerful message!

1 Before writing your words, consider your audience. Who is the best person to send your message to? Also, remember you'll need support. Who will support your message? The more people the better.

2 How will you create and send your words? You could pick from an email, letter, petition, video, blog, podcast, or something else you create. Think about which you can do best, and which will have the biggest impact. Remember that most things are done online now, but if you physically mail something, it could get to the right person more easily.

3 To create a powerful message, make sure to include the following: Describe the problem, explain it using evidence, persuade the reader to agree with your opinion, include facts, and propose solutions.

CHAPTER 6

> SAVING LIONS

AT TIMES I FEEL LIKE A CRUSADER FIGHTING TO ALLOW MANY DISTANT GENERATIONS TO BEHOLD A LION WALKING INTO THE RED DAWN AND ROARING RESOUNDINGLY."

—KAUSIK BANERJEE, LION RESEARCHER FOR WILDLIFE INSTITUTE OF INDIA

LADY LIUWA

For more than five years, Lady Liuwa lived alone. She roamed Zambia's vast Liuwa Plains—with no other lion in sight. A civil war in neighboring Angola devastated her homeland. During the war, soldiers and local people hunted zebra and buffalo to eat for themselves, and illegal trophy hunters killed most of Liuwa's lions. Others died of starvation. By 2003, Lady was the sole surviving lion.

After the war, the African Parks network moved in and protected Liuwa Plains and its small population of surviving animals. Soon, wildebeest herds multiplied. African Parks reintroduced other species back to the plains, too. But Lady remained alone. Then, in 2009, she got a big surprise. Two male lions from Kafue National Park in Zambia arrived at Liuwa. Lady quickly bonded with the males. Two years later, two younger lionesses joined the pride. African Parks staff hopes to glimpse baby lions soon. But one thing is clear— Lady is alone no more.

I t's not easy saving lions. Lions are large predators. They need a lot of open land to roam and plenty of big prey to eat. It takes hard work, cooperation, and a lot of money to keep lions alive.

HELPING LIONS IN INDIA

The Gir Park Authority in Gujarat, India, monitors the Gir Forest lions tirelessly. They manage the lions' habitat to make sure there's enough space and food for their prey. A special lion tracking team patrols the sanctuary, checking to see that the lions are healthy and safe. And the government punishes lion poachers.

Most importantly, the government supports the people living in and around the Gir Forest and Wildlife Sanctuary, where most of the lions live. The lion tracking team removes lions that become aggressive toward humans. And if a lion kills a farmer's livestock, the government pays the farmer for his loss. In return, local people support the lions.

The Asiatic lions' recovery has been so successful that about 100 Gir lions have migrated to three nearby forests—which the government also protects. But the Gir lions desperately need a second home, not only because they now overlap with humans, but also because a single disease outbreak or natural disaster could wipe out all the lions. The Indian government has grappled with this problem for years. The challenge is that large plots of land with no people and plenty of lion prey are hard to find.

In 2012, it looked like India finally found a solution to their problem. The Barda Wildlife Sanctuary is located about 124 miles (200 km) from Gir. Gujarat's Forest Department bred lion prey and dug ponds to create extra water sources for the new lions. They planned to move eight lions to Barda in August 2012, but a severe drought killed a lot of the lions' prey, and the plan was halted. There is still hope

LIONS ROLL ONTO THEIR BACKS AND EXPOSE THEIR BELLIES TO COOL OFF.

Lady Liuwa and her mate snooze together in the grass at Liuwa Plains National Park.

that Barda can provide a second home for the Gir lions, but for now the lions must wait for the sanctuary to replenish and recover.

Though Asiatic lions still risk extinction, the Indian government and the people of Gujarat refuse to give up. Many people hope Gujarat's success will inspire people in Africa to take more steps toward saving their lions. Several organizations and individual people work hard to convince local governments and villagers that sharing land with lions can benefit their communities.

A PARK FOR PEACE

People who don't live near wild giraffes, elephants, leopards, and lions will pay a lot of money to see them in the wild. This is called ecotourism. The money ecotourists pay to see these animals supports local communities. Local people get paid to be park rangers,

tour guides, and hotel employees. Ecotourists also spend money in nearby stores and restaurants, creating even more jobs for people. This is a win-win situation for humans and lions. If the lions and other large animals disappear, tourists will have no reason to visit these areas.

But there's plenty of excitement behind the ecotourism movement. Five countries in southern Africa recently launched a massive project to attract ecotourists. Angola, Botswana, Namibia, Zambia, and Zimbabwe cooperated to create a super park, also called a peace park. The park—which is bigger than the entire country of Italy—crosses into all five countries. It's called the Kavango Zambezi Transfrontier Conservation Area, or KAZA for short. It's the largest peace park in the world.

The president of each country signed an agreement

>> **LION SPOTLIGHT**

ON YOUR MARK! GET SET! GO!

Compare a lion's speed to their most popular prey.

Giraffe
(*Giraffa camelopardalis*)
35 MPH (56 KM/H)

Cape buffalo
(*Syncerus caffer*)
35 MPH (56 KM/H)

Elephant
(*Loxodonta africana*)
25 MPH (40 KM/H)

20 MPH
(32 KM/H)

THE BIG CATS INITIATIVE

National Geographic Emerging Explorer Luke Dollar spent much of his childhood trekking through a patch of rural Alabama woods near his grandparents' farm. Years later, Luke returned to the farm from college— but the woods and the animals that lived there were gone. The trees had been cut down and sold for timber. That sealed Luke's fate: He decided to follow his boyhood passion for wildlife. Today, Luke manages the grant program for the National Geographic Big Cats Initiative (BCI)—a group dedicated to saving large cats around the world.

A major BCI goal is to stop the decline of lions and other big cats and stabilize this magnificent predator's population before it's too late. The group funds critical lion, cheetah, tiger, and snow leopard conservation projects throughout the world where human–big cat conflict exists. So far the BCI has awarded more than $1 million to grantees that save lions, leopards, and cheetahs. As for their goal of halting lion and other big cat deaths, Luke is optimistic: "If you can conceive it, you can achieve it," he says. Check out the Big Cats Initiative at animals.nationalgeographic.com/animals/big-cats.

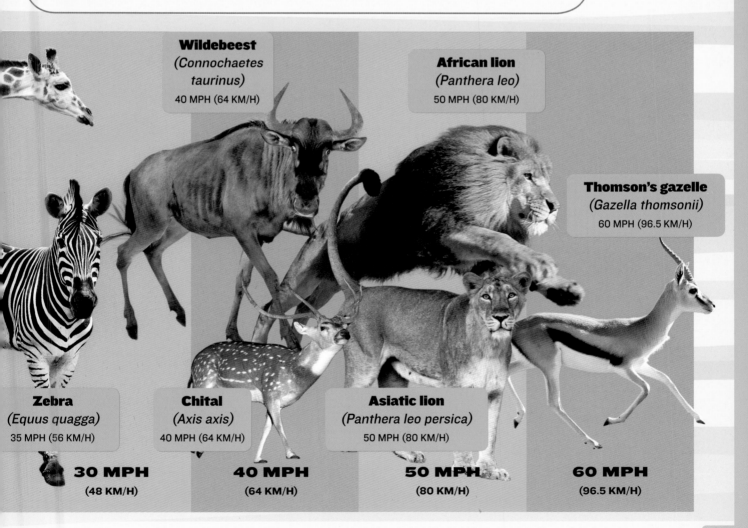

Wildebeest
(Connochaetes taurinus)
40 MPH (64 KM/H)

African lion
(Panthera leo)
50 MPH (80 KM/H)

Thomson's gazelle
(Gazella thomsonii)
60 MPH (96.5 KM/H)

Zebra
(Equus quagga)
35 MPH (56 KM/H)

Chital
(Axis axis)
40 MPH (64 KM/H)

Asiatic lion
(Panthera leo persica)
50 MPH (80 KM/H)

30 MPH
(48 KM/H)

40 MPH
(64 KM/H)

50 MPH
(80 KM/H)

60 MPH
(96.5 KM/H)

WHISKER NAMETAGS

The dotted pattern above a lion's whiskers is unique, like a human thumbprint. These whisker patterns help scientists identify individual lions in the field.

A friendly Maasai boy waves at a car full of tourists as it passes his home in Ndutu, Tanzania.

to protect the land and the animals inside the park, and to build eco-friendly hotels and restaurants for future tourists.

KAZA's success depends mostly on the 2.5 million people that live inside the park. That's a lot of people who need to be willing to share their backyards with large predators. KAZA includes 36 currently protected areas, but they are cut off from one another. KAZA's goal is to connect the protected areas with conflict-free open pathways, called corridors, so that the animals

>> ANIMAL RESCUE!

FILMING WILD LIONS

Captivated by the magical roars of lions at sunset, Dereck and Beverly Joubert moved from South Africa to Botswana 30 years ago. Now, they live among lions, filming them in their natural habitat. The Jouberts have spent thousands of hours sitting shoulder-to-shoulder in a rugged green safari jeep tracking the big cats. They've produced more than 20 films. One of those films—*Lions of Darkness*—triggered two decades of conservation victories that no one could have foreseen when the cameras started rolling.

The Jouberts showed *Lions of Darkness* to Botswana's president. He was so intrigued that he asked to see the three featured male lions up close, but the Jouberts delivered the sad news. No one could see the lions, because international safari hunters had legally killed them. The President was stunned. He quickly reviewed Botswana's lion hunting policies and asked the Jouberts for advice. Then, he took a drastic step. He lowered the number of lions that could be hunted each year in Botswana from 100 to only 8. A single film had instantly saved 92 lions. The Jouberts were elated. But they didn't stop. They continued to plead their case to save lions to Botswana's next two presidents. Finally, a few years ago, the government banned lion hunting for good. And in 2014, a new law will abolish all hunting in Botswana—a landmark victory for the Jouberts and Botswana's wildlife!

A Maasai warrior holds an antenna over his head to search the sky for a radio signal that will lead him to a collared lion.

MANY MAASAI PEOPLE LIVE IN HOUSES CALLED INKAJIJIKS MADE OF MUD, STICKS, GRASS, AND COW DUNG.

Above: A Maasai warrior visiting Highland Ranch in Colorado, U.S.A., teaches American students traditional songs and dances. Right: A boma reinforced with chain-link fencing and metal siding.

can safely travel in between. The corridors will allow animals to disperse their genes over a wider range and to continue to follow their annual migration routes to find food and water in the dry season.

WORKING TOGETHER

How do you keep a lion or a leopard from stalking and killing cattle along the corridors? And humans from killing the feline culprits in return? Today, many governments and nonprofit organizations work together across Africa to develop and run new programs that keep villagers, their livestock, and the lions safe.

The African People and Wildlife Fund (APWF) is a great example of this. The APWF works directly with Maasai warriors in Tanzania's Maasai Steppe. The Maasai Steppe is a massive area of woodlands and savannas—it's slightly larger than the U.S. state of

Maryland. One of Tanzania's most threatened lion populations lives there among humans.

The Maasai corral their cattle in pens, called bomas, at night. They pile cut thorn branches on top of one another to build the bomas, but lions often scale or break through the barriers to kill cattle. And the Maasai warriors retaliate. Working together, the APWF and the Maasai created a new type of boma, called Living Walls. They weave the thorny branches of local, fast-growing myrrh trees into sturdy chain-link fence to create a tall, unbreakable wall. The supplies to build the bomas are paid for partly by the Maasai and partly by donations from people around the world.

As I do a lot of community work in the Maasai Mara, the children and communities are all aware of my passion to protect lions and other wildlife. As a result they are starting to share my passion and will communicate with my team, all of whom belong to the surrounding communities, to let them know if a lion is endangered for one reason or another.

A Maasai herder stands with his sheep and goats inside a recently protected boma in the Mara.

>> EXPLORER INTERVIEW

ANNE KENT TAYLOR

BORN: ETHIOPIA
JOB: FOUNDER, PRESIDENT, AND CEO, ANNE K. TAYLOR FUND
JOB LOCATION: MAASAI MARA, KENYA, AND U.S.A.
YEARS WORKING WITH LIONS: 13
MONTHS A YEAR IN THE FIELD: 6

How are you helping to save lions?
By strengthening existing thorny livestock enclosures (bomas) belonging to the Maasai tribes who live in Kenya's Maasai Mara. These stronger fences prevent the lions from entering the livestock enclosures at night and killing the cows, sheep, or goats—and the Maasai from killing them in return.

Favorite thing about your job?
It allows me to spend a lot of time with lions and other wildlife in the wilds of the Maasai Mara. It also makes me feel happy that I am making a difference in the lives of animals by protecting and rescuing them as best I can.

Best thing about working in the field?
The privilege of being able to be amongst the wildlife in their natural environment. I find that we, as humans, can learn an enormous amount from watching animal behavior in the wild, where animals are not impacted by human intervention.

Worst thing about working in the field?
There really is not a "worst" thing for living or working in the field! There are definitely challenges and frustrations, but all of these can be overcome. Lack of communication and terrible infrastructure, with impassable roads, are a couple of the greatest challenges.

How can kids prepare to do your job one day?
I was fortunate to grow up in Africa. Other than that, I had very little preparation to do what I do in the field but always had a passion for wildlife and felt the responsibility to do whatever I could to keep them safe and from suffering. It is important to do things one step at a time. Otherwise the big picture can become overwhelming. It takes dedication and total commitment.

A young cub climbs on a broken tree limb in Botswana.

The APWF also created the "Warriors for Wildlife" program. Since the Maasai warriors are out on the Steppe every day and know the land intimately, the APWF pays them to help researchers track lion movements and record their behavior. This data will help governments create new conservation strategies.

The Warriors for Wildlife program is so successful that other nonprofit groups have spread out across Africa to set up similar programs, including in KAZA peace park.

The Zambian Carnivore Programme, for example, helps employ local people who work as scouts and scientists in several national parks across the country. The information they collect on lion populations, including the threats they face, helps protect the big cats and their habitats. They also remove poachers' snares that harm lions and other animals, and they treat domestic dogs that live near the parks to stop them from spreading diseases to lions.

HELP FROM AROUND THE WORLD

Many people work hard in Africa and India to help lions, but there's still a lot to be done. What if you don't live in lion territory? Can you still help save them? The answer is yes! You might not guess it, but many zoos donate part of the money they receive from entrance fees to organizations that work to save wild lions in Africa and Asia.

Another way to ensure lions' safety is to stop hunting them. In one effort to decrease lion deaths, several nonprofit groups in the United States teamed up.

These organizations gathered several pages of evidence detailing the challenges lions face. They wrote a letter to the United States government asking them to list lions as endangered under U.S. law. If a law passed, it couldn't stop people from hunting lions in Africa, but it would ban lion trophies (and other lion imports) from traveling back into the U.S. Hunters may think twice before paying thousands of dollars to travel to Africa to hunt lions if they can't bring back their trophy.

A lot of progress is being made, but we can't take the foot off the gas, or sit around and wait for other people to do the work. Saving wild animals is a never-ending job. It takes dedicated people living alongside them *and* people living far away.

A LION CAN TRAVEL MORE THAN 12 MILES (19 KM) IN A SINGLE DAY OR NIGHT.

>> RESCUE CHALLENGE

NOVICE

WORK WITH CATS

As you have seen, there are many different professions that work with cats and their habitats. Vets, conservationists, geographers, biologists, explorers, photographers, rangers, ecologists, wildlife police, campaigners, environmental lawyers, mappers, and fund-raisers are just a few of the professionals who help save lions.

For this challenge, you will need to take on the role of one of three different professions. Depending on where you live, you might be able to do this challenge with domestic cats or actual lions. To be good at any of these professions, you need to be good at asking questions. We have suggested some things you could ask when doing each job, but you should think of your own questions, too.

PROFESSION 1: FILMMAKER

Plan and record a short wildlife documentary about a cat. You could focus your story on a specific behavior, where it lives, and its relationship to other cats, or how it spends a typical day. If you can, use a computer to edit your movie and add narration.

When making your film question:
• Which cat are you going to film?
• What is the story that you are going to tell?
• Where is the cat and where does it go?
• When is the best time to catch it hunting, playing, sleeping, or eating?
• How are you going to film the cat?

EXTREME

PROFESSION 3: VET

Ask your local vet if you can work-shadow or event-volunteer with them for a day or more. As well as helping to feed and water any cats, ask if you can watch appointments when cat patients are diagnosed.

When helping the vet question:
• How are cats different from other animals?
• Which kinds of cats are most vulnerable to being harmed?
• Why do cats face different problems from other animals?
• How can vets help domestic and wild cats?
• What can you do to help sick or injured cats?

Lionkeeper Rebecca Kregar Stites's tips for studying lions:

1 Have a lot of patience. Lions spend the majority of their time resting, whether they live in a zoo or in the wild.

2 Practice studying lions in your local zoo. Start by trying to identify each individual. You will need a pair of binoculars so that you can find distinguishing marks such as scars and patterns.

3 Keep notes and have a camera handy so that you can snap a few photos to accompany what you have written down.

ADVANCED

PROFESSION 2: WILDLIFE BIOLOGIST

Observe a cat and keep field notes on its behaviors and what you think they might mean. It's a good idea to use a camera and pencils to sketch images of the behaviors that you identify.

When making your observations question:
• Where is the best place to observe the cat?
• What different behaviors can you observe?
• When can you see the different behaviors?
• How can you interpret what they mean?
• Why does the cat do what it does?

CHAPTER 7

>> TAKE ACTION

" IMMEDIATE AND MAJOR ACTION IS REQUIRED TO SAVE LION POPULATIONS IN AFRICA. "

— THOMAS E. LOVEJOY, BIG CATS INITIATIVE GRANTS COMMITTEE CHAIR

A lioness charges through water on a hunt in the Okavango Delta in Botswana.

Richard Turere is a sworn enemy of the lions that live near Nairobi National Park in Kenya, Africa. Richard is 11 years old. He stands guard over his father's cattle at night to protect them from predators. For two years, Richard has watched lions kill his father's cattle and he's fed up. Then, one night, it hits him. An idea. The lions slink out of sight when Richard shines his flashlight at them.

NAIROBI, KENYA 2011

Richard tracks down a solar panel and connects it to small, flashing lights. He positions the lights around the herd and flips the switch. Lions don't attack that night, and Richard sleeps soundly. His neighbors want Richard to rig flashing lights around their cattle corrals, too. Now Richard is saving his father's cattle from lion attacks, *and* he's saving lions from death by retaliation.

SAVING LIONS SAVES OTHER ANIMALS THAT LIVE IN LION HABITATS, TOO!

LEARN TO TAKE ACTION

Saving lions takes action. Richard Turere took action, and so can you. Depending on where you live, there are many things you can do to help save lions. Visit your local library to check out more books about lions, browse the Internet to find lion research, and watch documentaries to observe wild lion behavior. Then share what you learn with others. Lions can't talk, so you have to be their voice. Tell everyone you know about the challenges lions face.

If you're excited about saving lions, others will be too. Grab a friend and guardian and head to the nearest zoo. Zoos are a great place to learn about animals. Zoo animals are like species ambassadors—your personal link to wild animals. Hang out. Observe lions in their habitat. Hear them roar. How are zoo lions the same or different from the lions you see in the wild or in documentaries?

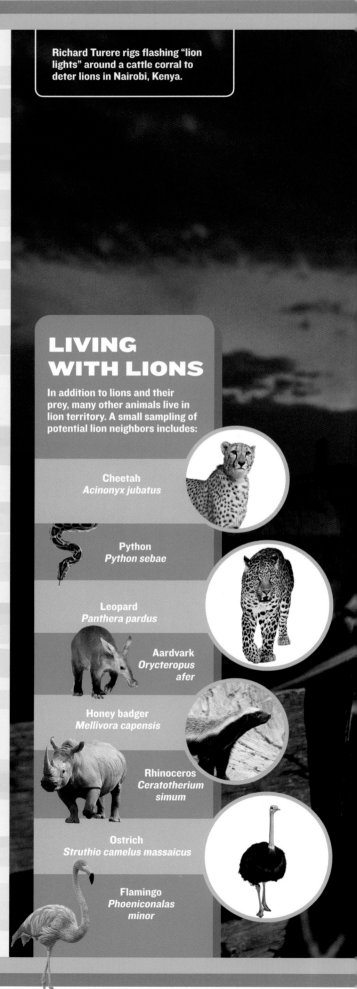

Richard Turere rigs flashing "lion lights" around a cattle corral to deter lions in Nairobi, Kenya.

LIVING WITH LIONS

In addition to lions and their prey, many other animals live in lion territory. A small sampling of potential lion neighbors includes:

Cheetah
Acinonyx jubatus

Python
Python sebae

Leopard
Panthera pardus

Aardvark
Orycteropus afer

Honey badger
Mellivora capensis

Rhinoceros
Ceratotherium simum

Ostrich
Struthio camelus massaicus

Flamingo
Phoeniconalas minor

Many zoos also have member programs like photo clubs and classes where you can go behind the scenes to learn even more about your favorite creatures. Explore your options!

Consider a career working with lions. Zookeepers feed lions and train them to be safe around people. Veterinarians give lions and other zoo animals check-ups and treat injuries. Some veterinarians even travel into the field with wildlife researchers to treat wounded animals or to safely attach tracking devices that collect important information about lions' lives.

Lion researchers spend several weeks or months a year in the field to study lions in the wild. They collect and analyze information about lions and recommend the best ways to protect them. Nonprofit organizations, like National Geographic, the African People and Wildlife Fund, and others featured in this book raise money and collect donations to protect critical lion habitat. They educate governments and local people about why wild lions are important. And they help pay for conservation programs.

If you live near wild lions, you can help teach others in your area about the importance of wild lions, too. Volunteer with a local nonprofit group, or start your own nonprofit and recruit others to volunteer. Be the next Richard Turere and brainstorm the best inventions you can think of to keep lions and humans safe.

Writers, photographers, and film producers help save lions by sharing their stories with others. National Geographic Explorers-in-Residence Dereck and Beverly Joubert have spent more than 30 years filming and photographing lions in the wild. Their stories inspire others to save lions. They live in Botswana literally in the lions' backyards! You could be a writer, photographer, or filmmaker too. Who would you share your stories with?

Saving wild lions takes action. And there's a lot to be done, so let's get moving!

>>> ANIMAL RESCUE!

KIDS 4 CATS

The Ruaha landscape in central Tanzania is a lion hot spot. About 10 percent of all the lions left on Earth live there—but human-lion conflict is high. As head of the University of Oxford's Ruaha Carnivore Project (RCP), Amy Dickman works together with other organizations and local communities to prevent lion deaths.

One very special program Amy runs is called Kids 4 Cats. Schools in the U.S. and U.K. pay money to "twin," or partner, with Tanzanian schools. The money pays for much needed supplies for local school children. So far the program has twinned seven schools—providing supplies for over 1200 children. As people in Ruaha see more benefits, their attitudes toward lions and other wildlife are changing. Lion deaths in the area have dropped drastically. Now, Amy and her team plan to expand Kids 4 Cats and other programs into neighboring communities, so even more people can receive benefits from living alongside lions.

Check out Kids 4 Cats and the Ruaha Carnivore Project at ruahacarnivoreproject.com.

Young lion cubs stick close to their mother as they travel through the Maasai Mara National Reserve.

BIG CATS IN ZOOS NEED HANDS-ON CARE TO KEEP THEM HEALTHY—INCLUDING TEETH CLEANING!

In 2012, filmmakers and National Geographic explorers Dereck and Beverly Joubert once again drove deep into the Duba bush. It had been two years since they last saw Ma di Tau and her young male cub. They found her looking stronger than ever. Still part of the Tsaro Pride, she was mothering a new set of cubs. A short while later, the Jouberts stumbled across a massive surprise.

It was Ma di Tau's young male cub! He had survived the toughest years of his life—and was looking very handsome.

The young male, whom the Jouberts have nick-named "Junior," is now just over three years old. He is growing into a full mane and has split from the Tsaro Pride. Soon, Junior will try to form a coalition with other bachelor males. One day the Jouberts hope to see him ruling his own pride.

The Jouberts are back in the field following Junior and other young males through their teenage years. The next film will reveal the secret lives of male lions on the move. In it, the Jouberts hope to answer questions like: Where do male lions go when they break away from the pride? How do they meet other males to form a coalition? And how do they prepare for a takeover?

Questions like these are important for lion conservation. Competition between lions will only increase as our human population continues to grow and place new pressures on them. Lions are calling on us to act—let's get out there and save lions!

Ma di Tau's male cub Junior all grown up in 2012.

>>RESOURCES

WANT TO LEARN MORE?
Check out these great resources to continue your mission to save lions!

IN PRINT

Carney, Elizabeth. *Everything Big Cats.* Washington, D.C.: National Geographic Society, 2011.

Divyabhanusinh. *The Story of Asia's Lions.* Mumbai, India: Marg Publications, 2008.

Hunter, Luke. *Cats of Africa.* Baltimore, Md.: The Johns Hopkins University, 2005.

Jackman, Brian, and Jonathan Scott. *The Marsh Lions: The Story of an African Pride.* Chalfont St. Peter, England: Bradt Travel Guides Ltd., 2012.

Joubert, Dereck, and Beverly Joubert. *Face to Face with Lions.* Washington, D.C.: National Geographic Society, 2008.

Joubert, Dereck, and Beverly Joubert. *The Last Lions.* Washington, D.C.: National Geographic Society, 2011.

Simon, Seymour. *Big Cats.* New York: Harper Collins, 1994.

ONLINE

African Lion Working Group
A group that works to support lion conservation
www.african-lion.org

Defenders of Wildlife
Protects animals and their habitats around the world
www.defenders.org

Government of Gujarat's Forests & Environment Department
Working to protect Asiatic lions
www.envforguj.in

Great Plains Conservation
A conservation group that supports ecotourism in Africa
www.greatplainsconservation.com

Gujarat State Lion Conservation Society
www.gujaratlion.com

IUCN
Information on the state of lions around the world
www.iucnredlist.org

National Geographic Education
Information about history, science, animals, and more
education.nationalgeographic.com/education

National Geographic Kids
Creature features give information on animals from around the world
kids.nationalgeographic.com/kids/animals

Wildlife Conservation Trust
Works to protect wildlife around the world
wildlifeconservationtrust.org

WATCH*

"Discovering the Secrets of Lions." *60 Minutes.* CBS News. November 25, 2012. (TV documentary)

Cave of Forgotten Dreams. Directed by Werner Herzog. Produced by Erik Nelson and Adrienne Ciuffo. 2012. (Documentary)

"The Desert Lions." *Nature.* PBS. Produced and directed by Amanda Barrett and Owen Newman. Scientific consultant, Dr. Philip Stander. 2007. (TV documentary)

The Last Lions. Directed by Dereck Joubert. 2009. (Film)

Lion Battle Zone. Produced by National Geographic Television for National Geographic Channel. 2012. (Film)

Lion Warriors. Executive produced by Dereck and Beverly Joubert. Produced by Kire Godal for Nat Geo WILD. 2010. (Documentary)

"Secrets of Survival: Life in the Namib Desert." *Nature.* PBS. Produced and directed by Amanda Barrett and Owen Newman. Scientific consultant, Dr. Philip Stander. n.d. Viewed online March 25, 2013.

The Pack. Produced by National Geographic Television for National Geographic Channel. 2010. (Film)

"The Truth About Lions." BBC Productions for BBC. Produced by Colin Jackson. 2011. (TV documentary)

*Most of these films and shows are available through various media, including TV, online, and DVD.

SELECT SCIENTIFIC PAPERS

Read about what scientists are doing today to protect lions:

Banerjee, Kausik, and Yadvendradev V. Jhala. "Demographic parameters of endangered Asiatic lions (*Panthera leo persica*) in Gir Forests, India." *Journal of Mammalogy* 93, no. 6 (December 2012): 1420-1430.

Banerjee, Kausik, Yadvendradev V. Jhala, and Bharat Pathak. "Demographic structure and abundance of Asiatic lions *Panthera leo persica* in Girnar Wildlife Sanctuary, Gujarat, India." *Oryx* 44 (April 2010): 248-251. doi: 10.1017/S0030605309990949.

Banerjee, Kausik, Yadvendradev V. Jhala, Kartikeya S. Chauhan, and Chittranjan V. Dave "Living with Lions: The Economics of Coexistence in the Gir Forests, India." *PLOS ONE* 8, no. 1 (January 2013). doi:10.1371/journal .pone.0049457.

Barnett, Ross, Nobuyuki Yamaguchi, Ian Barnes, and Alan Cooper. "The origin, current diversity and future conservation of the modern lion (*Panthera leo*)." *Proceedings of the Royal Society* (B) 273, no. 1598 (September 7, 2006): 2119-2125. doi:10.1098/rspb.2006.3555.

Divyabhanusinh. "Junagadh State and Its Lions: Conservation in Princely India, 1879-1947." *Conservation and Society* 4, no. 4 (December 2006): 522-540.

Henschel, Philipp, Dede Azani, Cole Burton, et al. "Lion status updates from five range countries in West and Central Africa." *CATnews* no. 52 (Spring 2010).

Joubert, Dereck. "Hunting behavior of lions (*Panthera leo*) on elephants (*Loxodonta Africana*) in the Chobe National Park, Botswana." *African Journal of Ecology* 44, no. 2 (June 2006): 279-281.

Lindsey, Peter Andrew, Guy Balme, Matthew Becker, et al. "The bushmeat trade in African savannas: Impacts, drivers, and possible solutions." *Biological Conservation* 160 (2013): 80-96.

Lobell, Jarrett. "New Life for the Lion Man." *Archaeology* 55, no. 2 (March/April 2012). archive.archaeology .org/1203/features/stadelhole_hohlenstein_paleolithic_ lowenmensch.html.

Loss, Scott R., Tom Will, and Peter P. Marra. "The impact of free-ranging domestic cats on wildlife of the United States." *Nature Communications* 4, no. 1396 (January 2013). doi:10.1038/ncomms2380.

Mosser, Anna, John M. Fryxell, Lynn Eberly, and Craig Packer. "Serengeti real estate: density vs. fitness-based indicators of lion habitat quality." *Ecology Letters* 12, no. 10 (October 2009): 1050-1060. doi: 10.1111/j.1461 0248.2009 .01359.x.

Nichols, Michael. "Zakouma Eye to Eye." *National Geographic*. March 2007.

Packer, Craig, A. Swanson, D. Ikanda, and H. Kushnir. "Fear of Darkness, the Full Moon and the Nocturnal Ecology of African Lions." *PLOS ONE* 6, no. 7 (July 2011). doi:10.1371/journal.pone.0022285.

Packer, Craig. "Rational Fear." *Natural History*. May 2009.

Riggio, Jason, Andrew Jacobson, Luke Dollar, et al. "The size of savannah Africa: a lion's (*Panthera leo*) view." *Biodiversity Conservation* (2013) 22:17-35. doi: 10.1007/ s10531-012-0381-4.

Singh, H.S., Gibson. L. "A conservation success story in the otherwise dire megafauna extinction crisis: The Asiatic lion (*Panthera leo persica*) of Gir forest." *Biological Conservation* 144, no. 5 (2011): 1753-1757. doi:10.1016/ j.biocon.2011.02.009.

Venkataraman, Meena. "Living with Lions." *Frontline* 30, no. 4 (Feb. 23-Mar. 08, 2013). Online www.frontline.in/ other/living-with-lions/article4431336.ece.

ORGANIZATIONS IN THIS BOOK

Anne K. Taylor Fund
For more information check out page 107.
www.aktaylor.com

Ewaso Lions Project
For more information check out page 35.
ewasolions.org

Global White Lion Protection Trust
For more information check out page 19.
www.whitelions.org

Kavango Zambezi Transfrontier Conservation Area
For more information check out page 93.
www.kavangozambezi.org

National Geographic Society Big Cats Initiative
For more information check out pages 43, 88, and 101.
animals.nationalgeographic.com/animals/big-cats

Panthera
For more information check out page 24.
www.panthera.org

Port Lympne Wild Animal Park
For more information check out pages 52 and 53. www.aspinallfoundation.org

Smithsonian National Zoological Park
For more information check out page 80.
nationalzoo.si.edu

University of Oxford's Ruaha Carnivore Project
For more information check out page 116.
ruahacarnivoreproject.com

University of Kent, Durrell Institute of Conservation and Ecology
For more information check out page 55.
www.kent.ac.uk/dice

University of Minnesota's Lion Research Center
For more information check out page 56.
www.lionresearch.org

Wildlife Films Botswana
For more information check out page 89.
www.wildlifefilms.co

Wildlife Institute of India
For more information check out page 64.
www.wii.gov.in

Zambian Carnivore Programme
For more information check out pages 20 and 90.
www.zambiacarnivores.org

Boldface indicates illustrations.

PLACES TO SEE LIONS AROUND THE WORLD

Bronx Zoo's African Plains, Bronx, New York
Denver Zoo's Predator Ridge, Denver, Colorado
Duba Plains (wild African lions), Okavango Delta, Botswana
Indianapolis Zoo's Plains Biome, Indianapolis, Indiana
Maasai Mara National Reserve (wild African lions), Narok County, Kenya
Port Lympne Wild Animal Park (Barbary descendants), Hythe, Kent, England
Sakkarbaug Zoo (Asiatic lions), Junagadh, Gujarat, India
Smithsonian National Zoological Park, Washington, D.C.

From page 7: $10.00 donation to National Geographic Society. Charges will appear on your wireless bill or be deducted from your prepaid balance. All purchases must be authorized by account holder. Must be 18 years of age or have parental permission to participate. Message and data rates may apply. Text STOP to 50555 to STOP. Text HELP to 50555 for HELP. Full terms: www.mGive.org/T

>> CREDITS

A.B.B.—

For Nicholas, intrepid leader of the Nash Pride.

The author would like to acknowledge:

Jennifer Emmett and Kate Olesin for asking me to write this book, and to the entire team at National Geographic Children's Books who helped make it possible—your talent and creative drive are inspiring.

Daniel Raven-Ellison, Dereck and Beverly Joubert, Luke Dollar, and all the explorers, researchers, and conservationists featured in the book—thank you for sharing your stories, photos, and expertise.

Kausik Banerjee for being my portal into the world of the Asiatic lion.

And all the passionate people around the world who study lions and work tirelessly to save them—this book would not have been possible without your efforts.

Published by the National Geographic Society
John M. Fahey, Chairman of the Board and Chief Executive Officer
Declan Moore, Executive Vice President; President, Publishing and Travel
Melina Gerosa Bellows, Executive Vice President; Chief Creative Officer, Books, Kids, and Family

Prepared by the Book Division
Hector Sierra, Senior Vice President and General Manager
Nancy Laties Feresten, Senior Vice President, Kids Publishing and Media
Jennifer Emmett, Vice President, Editorial Director, Children's Books
Eva Absher-Schantz, Design Director, Kids Publishing and Media
Jay Sumner, Director of Photography, Children's Publishing
R. Gary Colbert, Production Director
Jennifer A. Thornton, Director of Managing Editorial

Staff for This Book
Jennifer Emmett and Kate Olesin, Project Editors
Eva Absher-Schantz, Art Director
Lori Epstein, Senior Photo Editor
Em Dash Design, Designer
Ariane Szu-Tu, Editorial Assistant
Callie Broaddus, Design Production Assistant
Margaret Leist, Photo Assistant
Carl Mehler, Director of Maps
Sven M. Dolling, Map Research and Production
Grace Hill, Associate Managing Editor
Joan Gossett, Production Editor
Lewis R. Bassford, Production Manager
Susan Borke, Legal and Business Affairs
Moriah Petty and Cathleen Carey, Interns

Production Services
Phillip L. Schlosser, Senior Vice President
Chris Brown, Vice President, NG Book Manufacturing
George Bounelis, Vice President, Production Services
Nicole Elliott, Rachel Faulise, Robert L. Barr, Managers

The National Geographic Society is one of the world's largest nonprofit scientific and educational organizations. Founded in 1888 to "increase and diffuse geographic knowledge," the Society's mission is to inspire people to care about the planet. It reaches more than 400 million people worldwide each month through its official journal, *National Geographic,* and other magazines; National Geographic Channel; television documentaries; music; radio; films; books DVDs; maps; exhibitions; live events; school publishing programs; interactive media; and merchandise. National Geographic has funded more than 10,000 scientific research, conservation, and exploration projects and supports an education program promoting geographic literacy.

For more information, please visit nationalgeographic.com, call 1-800-NGS LINE (647-5463), or write to the following address:
National Geographic Society
1145 17th Street N.W.
Washington, D.C. 20036-4688 U.S.A.

Visit us online at nationalgeographic.com/books
For librarians and teachers: ngchildrensbooks.org
More for kids from National Geographic: kids.nationalgeographic.com

For information about special discounts for bulk purchases, please contact National Geographic Books Special Sales: ngspecsales@ngs.org. For rights or permissions inquiries, please contact National Geographic Books Subsidiary Rights: ngbookrights@ngs.org

Paperback ISBN: 978-1-4263-1492-6   Library ISBN: 978-1-4263-1493-3

Printed in China
13/PPS/1

Photo Credit Abbreviations: GI=Getty Images, IS=iStockphoto, MP= Minden Pictures, NG=National Geographic Creative, NGK=National Geographic Kids; SS=Shutterstock

FRONT AND BACK COVER: Beverly Joubert/NG **FRONT MATTER:** 1, Beverly Joubert/NG; 2–3, Anup Shah/Taxi/GI; 4–5, Beverly Joubert/NG; 6 (LE), Marina Cano Trueba/SS; 6 (INSET lo), SS; 6 (UP), Tim Fitzharris; 6 (LO), Karl Ammann/Digital Vision; 7 (LORT), Matthias Breiter/MP; 7 (UPRT), Darren Moore; 7 (UPLE), Lisa and Mike Husar; 7 (LOLE), Tim Davis/Corbis; 8–9, Beverly Joubert/NG; 10 (INSET), NGS; 10–11, Beverly Joubert/NG; 12–13, Beverly Joubert/NG; **CHAPTER 1:** 14–15, Beverly Joubert/NG; 16, Beverly Joubert/NG; 19, Karen-Jane Dudley/Barcroft Media/Landov; 20 (INSET), courtesy Matthew Becker; 20–21, courtesy Matthew Becker; 22–23, Ralph Lee Hopkins/NG; 24 (INSET), courtesy Philipp Henschel; 24–25, Beverly Joubert/NG; 26 (INSET up), Michael Fay/NG; 26 (INSET lo), courtesy Anne Kent Taylor; 26–27, Santanu Nandy/Flickr/GI; 28 (UPLE), lineartestpilot/SS; 28 (LO), Eric Isselée/SS; 28–29, Ansis Klucis/SS; 29 (UP), Karramba Production/SS; 29 (LORT), AtWaG/IS; 29 (LE), Elena Massimo Colombo/E+/GI; **CHAPTER 2:** 30–31, Beverly Joubert/NG; 32–33, Mauricio Anton/NG; 34–35, Chris Johns/NG; 35 (INSET), courtesy Ewaso Lions; 36, Jean-Philippe Varin/Science Source; 38 (INSET left), Beverly Joubert/NG; 38 (INSET right), Pete Oxford/MP; 38, Beverly Joubert/NG; 40 (INSET), Uri Golman/naturepl.com; 40–41, Uri Golman/naturepl.com; 42, Shin Yoshino/MP; 43, courtesy Pricelia Tumenta Fobuzie, Ph.D.; 44 (UP), Sergiy Nykonenko/IS; 44 (LO), ZUMA Press, Inc./Alamy; 44–45 (Background), Ansis Klucis/SS; 45 (UPLE), Simon Burt/Alamy; 45 (UPRT), Arterra Picture Library/Alamy; 45 (CTR RT), mediacolor's/Alamy; 45 (LO), Presselect/Alamy; **CHAPTER 3:** 46–47, Anup Shah/naturepl.com; 48–49, Beverly Joubert/NG; 50–51, Beverly Joubert/NG; 52–53, Gareth Fuller/PA Wire/AP Images; 54–55, Anup Shah/naturepl.com; 55 (INSET left), courtesy Milan Korinek/Olomouc Zoo; 55 (INSET right), Courtesy Simon Black; 56–57, Beverly Joubert/NG; 57 (INSET), Michael Nichols/NG; 58 (INSET), Theo Allofs/MP; 58–59, Beverly Joubert/NG; 60–61 (cat silhouettes), SS; 60 (UP), Odua Images/SS; 60 (LO), vblinov/SS; 60–61 (Background), Ansis Klucis/SS; 61 (UPLE), Dusan Zidar/SS; 61 (UPRT), Beverly Joubert/NG; 61 (LO), hartcreations/IS; **CHAPTER 4:** 62–63, Richard Du Toit/MP; 64, Mattias Klum/NG; 66–67, Sam Barcroft/Barcroft Media/Landov; 68 (INSET), Beverly Joubert/NG; 68–69, Beverly Joubert/NG; 70, Beverly Joubert/NG; 71, Michael Nichols/NG; 72–73, Des and Jen Bartlett/NG; 73 (INSET), courtesy Matthew Becker; 74–75, Pete Oxford/MP; 75 (INSET), Terry Andrewartha/npl/MP; 76 (UP), myrrha/IS; 76 (LO), Wild At Art/SS; 76–77 (Background), Ansis Klucis/SS; 77 (UPLE), Buena Vista Images/Photodisc/GI; 77 (UPRT), Mike Harrington/Taxi/GI; 77 (RT), unverdorben jr/SS; 77 (LO), Picsfive/SS; **CHAPTER 5:** 78–79, Brent Stirton/GI/NG; 80 (INSET), courtesy Rebecca Kregar Stites; 80–81, Dr. Jean Clottes; 82 (LE), Werner Forman/Universal Images Group/GI; 82 (UP), Joe Fox/Superstock; 82 (LO), Horizons WWP/Alamy; 83 (UP), Louise Batalla Duran/Alamy; 84–85, Radius Images/Alamy; 86–87, Lori Epstein/NG; 87 (INSET), Vanni Archive/Corbis; 88–89, Beverly Joubert/NG; 88, Mark Thiessen/NG; 90–91, Raul Touzon/NG; 90 (INSET), courtesy Matthew Becker; 92–93, Frans Lanting/NG; 92 (LOa), withGod/SS; 92 (LOb), Kitch Bain/SS; 92 (LOc), Anita Huszti/SS; 92 (LOd), Francois van Heerden/SS; 92 (LOe), Carmine Arienzo/SS; 93 (INSET), Andrea Capobianco/courtesy Michelle Kastern; 94 (UP), William Perugini/SS; 94 (LO), Vikulin/SS; 94–95 (Background), Ansis Klucis/SS; 95 (UP), NGK; 95 (LO), NGK; **CHAPTER 6:** 96–97, blickwinkel/Alamy; 98–99, Image Source/Alamy; 100 (A), gualtiero boffi/SS; 100 (B), saddako/SS; 100 (C), Four Oaks/SS; 101 (A), prapassong/IS; 101 (B), Eric Isselée/SS; 101 (C), Jeff Banke/SS; 101 (D), Corbis Premium RF/Alamy; 101 (E), Pete Oxford/MP; 101 (F), Stu Porter/SS; 101 (UP), courtesy Luke Dollar; 102 (INSET), Joseph H. Bailey/NG; 102–103, Randy Olson/NG; 103 (INSET), Mark Thiessen/NG; 104, Seamus MacLennan; 105 (UP), Dana Romanoff/NG; 105 (LO), courtesy Anne Kent Taylor; 106–107, Marcus Westberg/Life Through a Lens; 107 (INSET), courtesy Anne Kent Taylor; 108–109, Beverly Joubert/NG; 110, Monkey Business Images/SS; 111, Philip and Karen Smith/Iconica/GI; **CHAPTER 7:** 112–113, Beverly Joubert/NG; 114–115, Brent Stirton/GI/NG; 114 (A), Eric Isselée/SS; 114 (B), cellistka/SS; 114 (C), Eric Isselée/IS; 114 (D), Eric Isselée/IS; 114 (E), Meoita/SS; 114 (F), rusm/IS; 114 (G), Eric Isselée/IS; 114 (H), DaddyBit/IS; 116 (INSET), Verity Smith; 116–117, Anup Shah/naturepl.com; **CONCLUSION:** 118–119, Beverly Joubert/NG; 120, Eric Isselée/SS; 123, Beverly Joubert/NG